DAD, OLDE DAD

First published in 2019 by
Tamburlaine
3 Kilner House,
Clayton Street
London
SE11 5SE

Paul Bilic's right to be identified as the author of
this work has been asserted by him in accordance
with the Copyright, Designs and Patents Act 1988

Copyright ©Paul Bilic 2019

ISBN 978-0-954-16793-6

A CIP catalogue record for this book
is available from the British Library.

Typeset by Dominic Brookman
Printed in England by T.J. International,
Padstow, Cornwall

PAUL BILIC

DAD, OLDE DAD

TAMBURLAINE
2019

ONE
Olde Dad
1 – 12

TWO
Dad
13 – 65

British Travel Document – The Truth – The Two Birthdays – The Two Weddings – Dad's Trunk and Grannie – Embarrassed by him not wearing a Flat Cap – Ose for Sheep – My Dad's Hair – Emigrating to Australia – What were Foreigners doing with Pigs? – Uncle Joe – Hyde Wakes – Drago – The Two Wardrobes – Cha Cha Cha – Vernon Park – Stuffed Peppers – Frank Ifield – Is it worth learning to ride a bike? – My dad the protagonist. – Writing – The Seventies Photos – Houses – Other Boys' Dads – My Education – Laughing in Greece – Behind the Settee – Five Boys – Letting Go – Being Foreign – The Facts of Life – The Sporting Life – Aesthetic Positions – My Dad's English – What you are and what you once were – Dad's Wrist. – What my Dad didn't Know – Hitting me – A Little Death – Mollie's Parties – In the Pub – Der Verschollene – Mum's Death – An Insect Jig – The Man who went away – A Proper Watch – Sensory Deprivation – Killing a Fly – The Man who slowly erased himself – Peplums – Irish Christian Radio Stations – In the Ruins – Becoming a marionette

THREE
Olde Dad
66 – 81

FOUR
82. 171 Movies on Sky – 83. Jacqueline's Broken Glasses
84. In the Bed – 85. Translated

ONE

Olde Dad

1.

I am spending a week with my olde dad (91). It is a very hot day. Must be 26 degrees. I am sitting in our little square of garden on a deck chair. Half the garden disappeared when the extension was put in. Now there's just this bit. *What time is it?* I ask my dad. He is inside wearing a vest and thick shirt and thick socks, long-johns and a pair of thick trousers and heavy-duty slippers. It is about three o'clock. I'd dropped off in the deck chair after lunch. Dad says *Ah*. I repeat the question. The clock is in the house. *What time is it?* Dad says *Ah*. I can't see the clock from where I am on the deck chair. *What time is it?* This time he says *What type of what?* I repeat: *What time is it?* and point impatiently at an imaginary wristwatch on my wrist. This is not for anyone's benefit. He can't see me. *Ah!* he says after a minute (really, a minute!) He emerges into the garden. *It's a quarter to twelve.* I know it's not a quarter-to-twelve. *It's not a quarter-to-twelve,* I say. *How can it be a quarter-to-twelve. It was half-past-one when we had that salad.* My dad goes back into the house. *Ah!* He says. He comes out after about five minutes (really, five minutes!). *It's a quarter-past-three,* he says. Right. I've got the time now. That took about fifteen minutes. I get up and go in the house. Time to go out. I glance at the clock as I pass by. It's not a quarter-past-three. It's a quarter-to-three. Let that be a lesson to me. Next time just get up from the deck chair and go and look at the clock myself.

2.

I am going to cut my olde dad's toenails. My toenails are not great but his are really not great. *These toenails are not great,* I say. *Ah!* he says. *When did you last cut these toenails?* I ask. *Don't think I ever cut them,* he says. *You're ninety years of age,* I say. *You must have cut them at some stage. They're not that long,* he says. I have the big industrial nail-clipper but it still isn't easy. *Have we got a bowl or a bucket or something where you can soak your feet?* I say. *We must have,* he says, but can't think where it could be. In the end I find a plastic box that's being used to put pills in. I take all the pills out. *You could put some soapy water in and it could fit one foot. These feet are smelly,* I say. They are not clean. *Roll your trousers up!* We fit most of the foot in. With the bunion it's difficult. *I need a file,* I say. There's such a lot of stuff behind the toenails. This is not pleasant work. *You've got two good nails,* I say. *Good quality. But some of these others I just can't cut. They've grown into funny shapes.* They have and all. They have become like tusk, thick and twisted. One of them is the shape of a walnut whip. I can't get the clipper round them. They are like stone. *What I need is a barber for nails,* says my olde dad. *Chiropodists, they're called,* I say. *Next time you see the doctor, ask him to get you an appointment with a chiropodist. Ah!* he says. *I'll tell Helen,* I say. Helen is my sister. She lives with my olde dad full time. She's on holiday. That's one reason why I'm cutting his toenails today.

3.

Olde dad wants to buy a new electric razor and I said we can get one from *TK Max* at Crown Point North Shopping Centre. So that's today's trip. Each time I come home we get him one personal purchase. Last time it was trousers. Next time it'll be a new pair of underpants. At this rate by the time he's two hundred he'll have the full gentleman's wardrobe. When we get there I can only find so-called personal groomers and no electric razors. So-called Personal groomers trim your moustache and keep your facial growth apparent but optimal. They don't actually shave you. It can't be that there is a whole department devoted to personal groomers and no electric razors, can it? I ask a young man with a *TK Max* tag on. No. It's true. They don't do electric razors anymore. I can't believe it. So-called groomers but no electric razors! It's like putting the cart before the horse! I tell my dad there are no electric razors. He registers no surprise. We both need a sit down. We retire to the *Cafe Costa*. We get a small cappuccino each and he wants a chocolate cake with cream in it. A chocolate muffin comes closest. I watch as dad puts three sugars in his coffee. He is trying to open the fourth sugar. *You are NOT having four sugars in your coffee, dad,* I say. I noticed yesterday how much tomato ketchup he had on his pasta. *You eat like a Florida schoolboy,* I tell him. He smiles confusedly. It might be that he's thinking: that girl's got four songs on her i-pod; that bloke's got four apps on his smart-phone; I had four years in the Second World War; you've got four supplements on your Saturday bloody Guardian, you chattering class bastard. Now tell me I can't have another sugar in my coffee. *How's the coffee?* I say. *Creamy, isn't it?* He looks at me. *Too creamy,* he says.

4.

The plan was to get him playing chess again. He used to, about thirty years ago. So I sat him down and tried to get him interested. *It's all gone out of my head*, he said. *That's all right*, I said. *We'll put it all back into your head*. But I could see his eyes roving round, looking for a way out. His eyes rove around when he watches the telly now. They don't focus on it. The go looking for the bits of the room where the least is happening. Crannies and patches of empty air. After a minute he says he's got a headache and makes his escape. The chess plan is not going to work. Last night the lamp in his room stopped working. This was a big problem because he likes it on when he goes to sleep. In the end we just pulled the curtains back to let the lights of the street in. This morning I went to Morrisons and bought some bulbs but when we put one in, the lamp still wasn't working. He is fascinated by why it still isn't working and wants to show me how the electricity runs from the plug up the wire, up the lamp to the bulb. This bores me. My eyes start roving round looking for a way out. My eyes go looking for bits of the room where the least is happening. I can't fix wires. I come downstairs and start playing with the chess on my own. He stays upstairs and keeps looking at the probable route of current through the wires.

5

This morning about half-past-six the door to the bedroom where I am sleeping swings open and there is my olde dad. *You have to take me to the hospital,* he says. I am unfazed because I know this scenario. *What's up?* I say. *Everything,* he says. *Have a cup of tea and we'll see how it's going,* I say. This should work; it usually does. When I come down, it's 7.25 by the clock. *What time is it?* he says. *Seven o'clock,* I say, irritated. Seven o'clock in the morning in this house is like four in the morning in most houses. The day stretches out long and barren ahead. Dad talks me through what happened. *I thought I'll have a cup of tea. See how I feel.* If that's how you want to think about it, fine, I think. Though it *was* me who had suggested the cup of tea. I feel I want credit for this. A few minutes later he says, *did you say have a cup of tea?* I laugh. *Who else?* I say. *There's nobody else here. It's just you and me.* The cup of tea is a leitmotif that holds the day together. *Are you having a cup of tea?* he says whenever he has one. *I'm having coffee,* I say. *I don't drink tea in the morning.* It is now nine o'clock. I have said this ten times already. Still, it is a theme to embroider around. *You're having a mug this time,* I say. *I couldn't find the cup,* he says. I see the cup and saucer sitting forlornly on the kitchen top. *You didn't look very far. It's here,* I say. *I like a pot,* he says. Pot means mug, not teapot. This is in direct contradiction to what he usually says. It's good to articulate this so I say, *you always say you like a proper cup. Go way,* he says. Go way means rubbish. After a few minutes I sit in the extension bit of downstairs. I hear him clapping. He has taken to clapping loudly. At first I thought it was for attention. He told me it was because his hands went numb. I said he should take up boxing. *Go way,* he says. It's for attention too, I'm sure. When you get older you are ignored more, so you do what toddlers do for attention: Clap and want to see authorities like hospitals and doctors, and the next-door neighbour Paul, but I'll tell you about him another time.

6.

— Are you having a bath, dad?
— Nah.
— You should probably have one.
— I'll have one one of these days. Got too much on my plate at the moment.

I nod. *What are you up to today then?* Olde dad looks across to me, bemused by the question. It is as if we are in another time zone and what he had just said about having stuff on his plate isn't valid anymore. *What are you doing today then? We should have a walk,* I say. *Oh aye,* he says. *Got any errands to do?* I ask. *Food?* he queries, as though I had brought up the subject. *Food or anything,* I say. *Anything you need to pick up.* He looks bemused again, as if the idea that he actually did stuff was something out there in another galaxy, a galaxy to which, for reasons of propriety, we give ourselves no access. *You could have that bath later when we get back from our walk,* I say. My principle is keep nagging until it becomes a reality. *Too much on my plate,* he says. He probably has his principles too and they're keeping him out of that bath.

7.

My dad has never been what you call a swift walker. Even in the splendour of his middle age, the middle period of Illyrian swagger, even then his gait was unhurried. He has always been someone that refused to be hurried. He had a way of resting his hip mid-step, making the stride an elaborate double-action rather than the simple mundane shift of most people. These days it remains unhurried but is more of a painfully slow shuffle. When he is crossing the road he insists in engaging in one of his diagonal short-cuts, so that he is spending a good two minutes on the road itself. I play the role of watchful rook to his slow-motion bishop, scouting round for any vehicles as he performs his laborious hypotenuse. My dad is big on the short-cut. The one journey he does, to the shop to get his strawberry tart, has to be run through the tortuous labyrinth of his short-cut circuit, up behind Acre St, round alongside the primary school my mum went to eighty years ago and past the mildly futuristic elevation of St Mary's, the Seventies Catholic church. If you accompany him, you are not allowed to deviate from this route and must cross the roads always at the same places each time, usually diagonally. And don't bother with traffic lights. *You're too slow to cross without the lights*, I keep barking at him. *Yah!* he scowls back dismissively.

8.

There is a lot of time spent showing me the house, as though I am a potential buyer. *Come over here,* he says. *I want to show you this.* I get up from the settee and join him over by the front window. *Look at that,* he says. We look down through the house to the French windows at the back that were put in with the extension. *Yes, it's big now. There's a lot more space,* I say. *If you go into all these other houses on the street none of them are like this,* he says. *Have you been in any of the other houses?* I say. This confuses him a bit. *No, not for a long time,* he says. *But if you go in them you won't see any rooms like this.* I say he must be right. Later I'm by the French windows at the back and I say *it's getting nice out.* The sun has come out from behind clouds. *You do it like this,* he says and comes over to show me how to open the French windows, which was not what I'd wanted. I go out with him and he takes me the few paces across the now foreshortened garden to the back gate where he fiddles with the bolt. *Are you going out?* I say. *No. I'm just locking this gate.* The gate had been locked. He is now unlocking it. Then he locks it again. A lot of his time, I have noticed, is spent unlocking locked doors to lock them again more securely, readjusting curtains that were in the right place to keep the sun out and then having to re-readjust them, switching a light on, then off, then on again, turning a dial to where it shouldn't be before returning it back to where it had been. He is reliving the moment that secured something, enjoying the surety of that instant. *You just slide it in like this,* he says half to me and half to himself, as he jams the bolt across. I nod and utter a reassuring grunt.

9.

We went to the bank. There has been much confusion because my dad has two bankbooks from the *Halifax* (he won't do bankcards). One bankbook has quite a lot of money on it. One less. I said, *they're putting your pension money into the bankbook with a lot of money, dad.* He insisted they weren't. His reasoning seemed to be that because he was using the other one to take money out, that was where the pension was going. *But this one's got no deposits in it, dad, just your withdrawals,* I said. *Go way,* said olde dad. So we had to go to the *Halifax* to get it confirmed by an eighteen year old teller. The bank is the authority. I know nothing. I remember a few years ago we went to see my sister Liz on the other side of Manchester. We had to take the tram back to the centre of Manchester. *Are you sure we're going the right way?* he said *This is the only way, dad. We just follow the line. It's a tram. It can't turn off and go down a back street.* This wasn't enough for him. He went round asking people on the tram if we were going the right way. *There's only one way, mate.* And then there's the next-door neighbour Paul. At the slightest confusion dad wants to knock on his door and bring him in. *How do you switch the oven on?* I asked once. *I'll just have a look, dad.* Olde dad said *I'll go and bring Paul in. No,* I said. *Paul's got his own family, dad. He doesn't want you bothering him.* I'm too late. He's out the door and comes back with Paul. And then he asks him for the number of a quote qualified electrician unquote for the lamp. I've told him an electrician will cost £100 to come out. *We can buy another lamp like this for £10. Go way,* says dad. I look at Paul. Paul gives his assent. That's all right then. We won't call the qualified electrician. Paul the neighbour is now the biggest Paul in dad's life. He keeps calling me David anyway. David's my brother. The other day he actually said it. *Which one are you? I'm Paul* I said. *Go way!*

10.

What's it doing out? I say. Dad is sitting in his chair looking out of the window. He says he likes that chair because he can see out. From the angle he can just see the sky and the top of the house opposite, but he can see weather, which is the main thing. *Not doing anything at the moment,* he says. *Not spitting?* I say from the kitchen as I put my eyes in (contacts). Dad has already put his teeth in. He does that in his chair. He is going to pop out to *Bargain Booze* to get some more milk for his honey hoops. *Isn't there enough in the fridge?* I say. *What?* he says. *Milk. Isn't there enough in the fridge?* I say. *I need some for honey hoops,* he says. *But isn't there enough in that carton in the fridge? You put too much in yesterday remember and had to throw it down the sink,* I remind him. *What?* he says *Milk,* I say. *Yesterday you put too much in and had to throw it down the sink, remember. Go way,* he says. Dad is putting his gear on. Jacket, shoes with velcro fastener, cap. *Have you got your glasses? What?* he says. *Have you got your glasses on?* Dad goes round to find them. There are a collection of different glasses throughout the house that must mostly belong to people who are not here this week and then there is dad's reading glasses as well as his distance glasses.
Ten minutes later.

— Have you got the right ones?
— What?
— The right glasses.
— Don't know.
— What are those ones there?
— Who put them there? says dad.
— Don't look at me, I say. What's it doing out?
— Not doing anything at the moment, he says.
— Not trying to spit, I say.
— Nah, he says dismissively.
— Got some change? I say.

He is rummaging through a coat pocket where he keeps coins. *Take an umbrella,* I say. He makes a quiet guffaw.

For some reason, he has never liked umbrellas. They are something ridiculous
— That way, if it rains you put it up.
— Go way.
He's out the door.

11.

We are going out for a walk in the direction of the shops. There is no particular errand to run but olde dad will buy a strawberry tart for his stock in the fridge. At the shops olde dad decides to buy some chocolate bars in the newsagents. I go in with him and think I might buy a paper. On the outside of the shop it clearly said *newsagents* and *The Sun* in bold Sun-red with a slogan like *The Home of News* or something, but in the shop there are no newspapers. *Got any papers left?* I say. *No Suns left*, says the newspaperman. That's it. There were only Suns anyway.

On the way back olde dad is fretting about something.

— I thought I had some change, he says.

— Why? Didn't you have any?

— Was sure I had some.

— So, did you have to pay with a note?

I know he carries a wad of £20 notes around with him. I've warned him about this. *Somebody'll nick them*, I say. *Go way*, he says.

— You bought that thing yesterday for £17. You should have £3 left from that.

I know he bought something for £17 yesterday but it seems to be a secret what it was, perhaps because it was £17, which is a lot of money and therefore unspeakable.

— But you must have spent that on the strawberry tarts, I said, trying to unravel the mystery of why he had to break into a fresh £20 note.

— No. I didn't.

He is feeling in his pockets for change.

— I was sure I had some change, he says.

— Well, if you spent it on the strawberry tarts you wouldn't have anything left for the chocolate, would you?

He is still feeling around in his inside jacket pocket.

— You would have had three pounds left from that thing yesterday and you spent that on the strawberry tarts and so that's why you've got no change left for the chocolate.

He is still pulling a face.

— You should just take one £20 note out with you, I repeat, nagging him remorselessly. We are crossing over by the Catholic church on his little circuit.

— So, did you have to break into another £20 for that chocolate? I ask again, not letting it go.

— No.

— Well, how did you pay then?

— I had some change.

— But you said... oh never mind.

I stride on ahead. I've had enough.

12.

We are sitting in the bit of garden left over after the extension. It has cleared up since this morning. Dad says, *see that hedge. A few years ago it was thin and little. I could talk over it and see through it.* I look at the hedge. It is dense and about nine feet high. *Yes,* I say, *it's all grown over.* Then I say, *you know I'm off tomorrow. Ah,* says dad. *I'm taking the train. But David's coming on Friday, so you'll only be on your own one night. Oh,* he says, *you'll have to stay another night. I can't,* I say. *I've got my ticket now.* I know this works best; the material trumps everything. *You'll be all right for one night. Then David's here for the weekend. Then Liz is back from Italy on Monday and she'll come and pick you up and you'll be at her house for a couple of weeks till Helen comes back and it's back to normal again.* He likes normal. Remember your glasses and your pills and everything, won't you, when Liz comes to get you. I shouldn't have said that. He starts to fret about everything he'll have to remember. When I came here a week ago I thought I'd write a blog post and call it *Egg and Chess* because I wanted to get dad playing chess and get him eating egg. I thought that'd be good for him. He soon put me right on that: didn't want to be taught chess and didn't like eggs. Fair do's. We are looking at the hedge, which is mature and tangled, formidable really. *Do you want an ice cream?* I suggest perkily. *No,* he says and looks somewhere else, somewhere where there's nothing much to look at.

TWO

Dad

13.

British Travel Document

The British Travel Document for stateless people is apparently red now, probably very similar to the usual passport colour, the passport you get if you are a British citizen. It used to be pink, though a part of me remembers it as white. Dad had to get one of these stamped if he wanted to go abroad. He went abroad twice. Once to visit me in Paris. For this he and my mum went to Liverpool to get a stamp. And once to go to Greece to my sister's wedding. For this one I went to Croydon where there was the office for foreign nationals or something like that at the time. I don't know. It may still be there but I have no cause to go there now as olde dad won't be travelling anymore if he can help it. He must still have the stateless travel document somewhere in a drawer or in an old jacket pocket. There is a secret place where he stores all his confidential things. His bank books and a copy of his last will and testament, I shouldn't doubt. The travel document will certainly be there, doubtless now out of date.

Dad once applied to become a British citizen but they refused him, though they said if you try again in a couple of years we'll probably give it you. Dad didn't bother. It cost too much. At one stage official documents referred to him as a dissident, which sounded glamorous, but they soon resorted back to stateless person, which was probably closer to the truth.

14.

The Truth

It's hard to get at the truth. Histories don't tell it. When the Second World War started my dad in his village in Dalmatia, in an area called Krajina in a Serbian enclave in Croatia, fought for the king against the Communists and against the Nazis. When you asked dad where he was from what he always said was Dalmatia. He was also what they called a četnik. For the British with their simple lines of good and evil this is complicated. I don't even know if my dad realized who he was fighting for and why. He was a teenager. But he was married and his wife was pregnant. Then, for whatever pressing reason, he had to flee. The Communists under Tito had won. They had been supported by the Soviets and by the Allies who wanted to stand side by side with the Soviets for strategic reasons. Dad left the country, marched day and night to escape. When he escaped he was put into a camp for displaced people. He was now stateless and could not return to Dalmatia. At the end of the war he spent a number of years in transit camps in Germany and, mainly, in Italy, in Calabria. They were all waiting to be given a place to go to. They were expecting it to be America. It turned out to be England. In fact, he was shipped to Wales, near Swansea, where he had to stay in the camp for a period of, I don't know, six months or so, before being given the right to go where he wanted. When he got the chance to move freely, he went to Manchester which was an industrial centre where he had heard there might be work. His wife with his unborn child was now years away. How well had he known her anyway? This is mysterious. Once or twice I tried broaching the question but it was difficult and olde dad seemed to have forgotten; it was all so long ago, another life. These things will never be known.

15.

The Two Birthdays

Olde dad was born in 1924, though there is some doubt about the actual date of birth. My mum told us that once, having initially told her that his birthday was some time in November, one day, some years after, he changed his mind and said it was actually May 23rd. *How can you not know your own birthday?* she said. Dad explained that the November birthday had been his brother's birthday. It was too late for official documents, though. He'd already given the brother's birthday, and the feeling was that the authorities would not comprehend the error, as indeed my mum couldn't. Many years later, just a few years ago, when I took olde dad to Stepping Hill hospital to see the eye doctor and the doctor asked him his birthday, olde dad, quick as a flash, came out with this date, November 17th or whatever. I looked at him confused, before remembering the anecdote of the two birthdays. He still remembered the date of the official birthday. It must be one of the necessary lies he carries around with him for the alien exterior world. And these responses, learnt so well they have become instinctive, will be the last thing he lets go of.

16.

The Two Weddings

After my mum died in 2001 my sister took me aside and told me the secret that dad had confided to her. He had expressly said that my brother David and I should not be told this secret. When dad had met mum and they wanted to get married all those years ago they couldn't because my dad was already married in Dalmatia. So what they did was they went to Blackpool for the day and came back and told everybody that they'd got married. So then they started living together and had babies (us) and did the family stuff. Then years later, after (I presume) some negotiations with Yugoslavia as it then was, there was a divorce and they could legally get married. So they went to Blackpool on a day trip again and got married without telling anybody. They left us kids with Uncle Joe and Auntie Peg, which explained why there were never any photos of their marriage. We had photos of all my mum's sisters getting married and photos of my grannie getting married again to Jack Archer in the 1970s or whenever but nothing of their own wedding day. Anyway, when my mum died, dad was scared that if he died and we all looked at documents and papers we'd see that they got married in the 1960s and be confused, so he told my sisters, though expressly said that me and David shouldn't be told. Nobody knew. It was a great secret from grannie and all my mum's sisters (even Peggy), all older than her, who would never have accepted them living together out of wedlock. They were liberal without wanting to be, mum and dad. I don't know who came up with the Blackpool plan. Probably my ingenious mum. Two birthdays and two marriages. That must be a record.

17.

Dad's Trunk and Grannie

Before they got married (or pretended to get married) my mum and dad lived with my mum's mum probably in Gorton (most things were in Gorton). This was my grannie Florie. My dad, being a foreigner, was under suspicion most of the time. He had a trunk in which he kept any worldly goods he had. Florie took my mum aside and voiced her suspicions. She thought he had a dead body in there. One thing he did have in there was his English dictionary, a tattered black-covered tome that I remember seeing on our shelves when I was a boy. One day it was so dirty and tattered my mum threw it out. I remember my dad saying *where's my dictionary?* And my mum told him she'd thrown it out. It was probably one of the only things he had left from those days. On another occasion, and on the other hand, I remember my mum being upset after she came home one day and dad had torn down the rose bush that crept up the wall at the bottom of the garden. She said *sometimes when I'm in a bad mood and I look out and see the roses it's the only thing that cheers me up and now he's torn it down.* So tit for tat. Dictionary for a rose bush. Florie died when she was ancient at about seventy-three or so and I was about eleven or twelve. She had started wandering off from the house in Gorton where she lived with Jack Archer, second husband. She probably had Alzheimers. I remember being looked after by her in that little house in Gorton near Belle Vue and having to play *hunt the thimble* with the area of play being limited to the mantlepiece. You had to hide the thimble on the mantlepiece and then someone had to look for it. Not a great game for a hyper-active seven-year-old. When she was angry she'd say things like *look sharp or your mother'll be vexed,* expressions from the nineteenth century, almost it seemed to me out of Dickens. When she died I remember Auntie Peggy and Auntie Molly, older sisters, coming round together to tell my mum. I had never seen them arrive together before. It was like they were ganging up on her. They came round because they both had phones and we didn't have a phone. As the youngest sister mum had stayed at home alone with her mum for longer, so she was closer to her. Also Molly and Peggy had both got married young when they were about eighteen. My mum didn't get married till she was twenty-six, practically an old maid in those days.

18.

Embarrassed by him not wearing a flat cap

At primary school, if ever my dad came to pick me up, I was always slightly embarrassed by him not wearing a flat cap and not looking like an old man. He was also foreign, of course, and in those days in Manchester suburbs, in Stockport, there weren't that many foreigners around. When you're little you mainly want to be like everyone else. I remember him coming to pick me up from school one day. I don't know why he came to pick me up. Normally I went home on my own on the school bus. There would have been a period when I was the only one at St Joseph's. David would have gone on to grammar school and Helen and Liz wouldn't be at school yet. So it must have been in that period when I was seven. I remember being surprised that he'd managed to get there. I didn't know he knew how to get there. It had always been my mum who did the domestic things. My dad just went to work and came back at odd times because of the shift work. Anyway, this time it was him and he emerged as though out of context in my school playground to pick me up, doing a job somehow unsuited to him. It was like the time my mum was in a bad mood and refused to cut my hair and said *Why doesn't your dad do it?* She must have been fed up with him. So I said to my dad *You do it,* taking her at her word. She must have meant it as a rhetorical question. So he took the scissors and took a snip. Mum intervened immediately. He had taken a great chunk of hair out in one snip. It must have made mum realize. You couldn't trust him with stuff like that. Though this time at St Joseph's there he was, bold as brass with his big, good looks, surrounded by other parents, mostly mothers, the men mostly being Irish working men (this was a Catholic school) and older English men in flat caps with no teeth already. I put my hand in his. He had huge hands with great thick sausage fingers.

19.

'Ose for sheep

I remember when my mum used to talk about how it had been with dad when they first met. *It was a terrible time*, she said. No Irish, foreigners, blacks or dogs allowed in buildings and mum going out with a foreigner. Her trying to understand his accent. Once she asked him what he did for work and he told her. He made *'ose for sheep*. She couldn't make head or tail of it. 'Ose for sheep. *But why didn't you ask him to explain?* we asked. *You couldn't*, she said. *He had a terrible temper*. He would have lost his temper so she pretended to understand. All foreigners had terrible tempers. It was only some time afterwards that she'd understood what he did. He made hose for ships. My dad, as I remember writing on my university application form many years later, was what was called a plastic tube extruder, which meant that he took plastic tubes out of a machine. He minded that machine and had a relationship with it. He did that all his working life in Manchester, first in Trafford Park and then in Romily near Stockport. At the time my dad met my mum he would have been a glamorous foreigner. There is a black and white photo of him from the time sitting on the grass in Piccadilly Gardens Manchester, stretched out like a pasha as if he owned the place. He must have been remarkably exotic to my mum, who was good-looking herself with her blue eyes and black hair. They were quite a glamorous couple. I remember when I was about twenty and I don't know who it was, one of my mum's colleagues maybe (my mum worked in the chemist of the big co-op in Stockport town centre), had said I was good-looking, and I remember my mum immediately piping up to say how my dad had been properly handsome. Now he *was* good-looking, she said.

20.

My Dad's Hair

My dad has always combed his hair back to reveal his forehead. It's kind of what I do with my hair now. When I was a teenager my dad would have been the age I am now more or less. His hair like mine was mainly dark (his black, mine dark brown) but greying heavily at the temples. I have inherited the exact pattern of hair evolution from him, as I have his back, his nostrils, his mouth. His hair strategies must have seemed good ones to me from an early age. My brother David, on the other hand, has never imitated dad's hair strategies. As in so many things, he went his own way. I remember one time – it must have been round about this time when my dad was in his early fifties – he used to put brilliantine on his hair. We didn't know what it did but the idea that he was trying to dye his hair seemed shameful to us. I remember thinking it was ridiculous, like Gustav Von Aschenbach in *Death in Venice* putting eye-shadow and lipstick on to make himself appealing to a young boy. I didn't like the idea of my dad looking after his appearance. When he had varicose veins and went for an operation to get rid of them I remember saying *what's he having the operation for? It doesn't matter.* My mum, quite rightly, shouted at me, saying *of course he should have the operation. It wasn't nice for him to have them.* Like so many selfish kids with their parents, I didn't like the idea that they took an interest in their own appearance.

21.

Emigrating to Australia

In Manchester in the sixties and seventies the main question for all working-class families was always *shall we emigrate to Australia?* Australia was a sun-drenched land where, mainly, *their winter was like our summer.* I don't remember all this very well, but I remember my mum telling me that we did apply to emigrate to Australia or it may have been Canada and the process was moving forward. What she said was that one day she had a visit from the home office and a man told her that the UK wanted to keep families like ours with four young children in the country and would she reconsider her decision? So she did and we never went. I find it very difficult to believe that an official, wherever he was from, would come out of his way to visit some anonymous family. Like a few things that my mum said over the years, I wonder if she hadn't imagined this. A man coming from out of nowhere, a man in a suit, I imagine. So we never went to Australia as three of my mum's brothers and sisters had done: Uncle Jack, Auntie Nellie and Uncle Billy, Jack and Billie dying young as most working-class men did, cigarettes doing for Jack and alcohol for Billy, leaving four sisters, Mollie the eldest, Nellie, Peggy and my mum the youngest Kath, the one who married a foreigner.

22.

What were foreigners doing with pigs?

Sometimes, in an attempt to get at the truth about olde dad, how he had been as a young man, I asked him about things. What did you do when you were in, say, Wales? Once I got a story out of him. He and some of the other men in this camp in Wales had bought a pig from a local farmer and they were killing it in a village to then cook it and have some good pork. Natural behaviour for people used to rural mountain living in the Balkans in the 1940s. British villagers stopped them and they were, astoundingly to them, prohibited from slaughtering this pig. I remember telling this story to my Auntie Molly many years ago and she looked back at me uncomprehending, her mouth open in horror and asked, somewhat haughtily, *What were foreigners doing with pigs?*

I imagine my dad as a 25-year-old man engaged in this story. It is difficult to see it as anything other than a Sunday evening BBC drama, a light-hearted, nostalgic look back at more innocent times highlighting charming foreigners, uptight and mostly comic British. There would be a love story between a pretty Welsh girl and a dashing foreigner. My dad could have that role. At some stage something serious would crop up. The threat of repatriation, imprisonment. It would end happily with a leap forward to a few years later and a litter of kids and a stable family at the heart of the Welsh community. Well, it wasn't very far away from what happened. Except that the foreigner went to Manchester and met someone there. There were kids, except that they were manipulated into the community by various trips to Blackpool. They lived happily ever after. I suppose so, except that the past, the memory of that other life and what to do with it, would always been an extra complicating element that meant it could never fit the Sunday evening schedules.

Uncle Joe

Uncle Joe had given me humbugs, Blackpool rock, sugared almonds, chocolate dragees, raspberry ruffles, jaffa cakes, cough candy, ice cream. I had done the things that children do: shown off; told tall tales; fallen over a lot; been wholly, unselfconsciously engaged with the material world. These things were not particular to me. They were the lot of all children. I had been a child at a particular moment in time and space, and Uncle Joe had been Uncle Joe at a particular moment too. That had been our connection.

As I grew older, left home, our meetings became less frequent. Each time I went home to see mum and dad, I went to see Uncle Joe and his adjunct wife Auntie Peggy. Auntie Peggy sat next to him on the settee, her knees pointing in his direction and echoed his sentiments, backing him up like a valiant ensign. Uncle Joe held forth like a pirate of the High Seas with Gorton and Ardwick as his stomping ground, always Gorton and Ardwick, as if passing beyond their frontiers of East Manchester you fell off the edge of the world. His purple rhetoric of voice and gesture brought his humble tales of old Gorton haunts and famous — to me unknown – personalities he had met in his picaresque navigations of the inner city into the realm of myth. Uncle Joe was an artist in his own small unmarketable field, a storyteller with no real material but a fabulous control of the form: the thumb jab out left to indicate an ancillary character emerging into the story; the rise and fall of intonation; the pregnant pause with only the clink of tea time crockery to mitigate it; the knit and cast of brow and eye beam. Uncle Joe was the king of the living room.

People are unknowable; we know that. Even people who resemble you, with the same experiences, the same background, class index, cultural cladding. Your siblings;

your best friend; your lover. They are all fretting day and night about stuff you are not party to. Uncle Joe was further out from my orbit than this. He was a distant cloudy nebula. He was from another world, one couched in smoke and mist, the fuzz of black and white photos and dark grey crannies. Photos of Uncle Jo were like photos by Nadar, the great nineteenth century photographer, as though conjured up by the flash of the bulb, magical and smelling of gunpowder. His world; his head; the thoughts that careered through the runnels of his mind and the instincts that sparked within its cavernous brainscape: it was all unfathomable.

24.

Hyde Wakes

Now and again Joe and Peg would come round and take us all out. One time I remember we went to Blackpool and had a picnic with sausages. I can't remember how they were heated. It must have been a kind of camping-gas affair. We sat amongst the sand dunes. The event is recorded on Joe's home movies. I remember the flies buzzing round us as we tried to eat the sausages. Another time they took us to Hyde wakes. Hyde is just next to Denton where Joe and Peg lived and the wakes happened for a week in, I think, the autumn. I think it was a school day because I remember being astonished and delighted that they could come round and just whisk us away to the fun fair like that, and feeling sorry for my mum and dad who were left at home as there would be no room for them in the car. Of course, that was probably it. We were taken out so that they could have some time alone together. That was why we were taken to Blackpool for the day, why we were taken to Hyde wakes. There must have been a conversation where my mum said it would be nice if they could have a break from the kids and Peg said *we'll take them to Blackpool or to Hyde wakes*. When you are little you cannot imagine that your parents want time away from you, that they don't love that their whole life revolves around their four snotty children. It did not occur to me what they could get up to without us. As I imagined, they would just be talking about the same things, doing the same domestic chores, but without us there to complete the event, to make it whole. As it was, who knows what they talked about? Them? Their relationship? I doubt it. This was a working-class couple in the early Seventies. I don't think the concept of their relationship occurred to them. So maybe they just breathed in the quiet of a childless space for a few hours, or just watched *The Two Ronnies* as usual but without us being there.

25.

Drago

In the late sixties (I know it was the late sixties on account of the colour photos and the haircuts that everybody had) Drago came to our house. Drago was dad's son from Yugoslavia whom he had never seen. We knew dad had another son and I remember my mum telling me he was my half-brother. Drago and dad spoke Serbo-Croat together. We didn't speak Serbo-Croat. My mum had thought that it would be a bad idea speaking a foreign language, that it would put us at a disadvantage in relation to other children. My dad himself never spoke the language apart from when we went to Halifax once a year to visit Dušan and his wife Militsa and their son Milan. Dušan had come over with my dad from the camps and had somehow started working in Halifax. Militsa worked for Macintosh's chocolates and always gave us an enormous bag of *Quality Street* each. Apart from in Halifax dad never spoke Serbo-Croat. Later in life when there was a phone call from Belgrade once a year from Drago or from dad's brother Milan or his sister Maria, dad had trouble finding his words. Once he told me that he didn't know the word for aeroplane. It wasn't a word he knew about as a boy. When Drago came to see us we did special trips. We went to London for the day, four of us, dad, Drago, David and me. My mum stayed at home to look after the girls. At that stage mum had never been to London. I don't think she was happy that we were all going on this trip to London and she was stuck at home still. I don't blame her. Or maybe it was her idea for us to go to London for the day. There are black and white pictures of me and David sitting on a canon near The Tower of London. I don't know why these photos are black and white while the ones of Drago at our house were colour. The one thing I remember is dad going to buy us some ice cream and then learning it was two shillings or maybe half a crown for an ice cream, in any case way more expensive than in Stockport, and getting angry and saying we couldn't have one. So David and me and Drago, dad's first son he had only just met, went without an ice cream on our day trip to London.

26.

The Two Wardrobes

In my mum and dad's room there were two wardrobes: mum's wardrobe and dad's wardrobe. They had always been there since I can remember. They must have been bought together as a set as they were made out of the same type of wood or imitation wood. They were identical except that mum's wardrobe had a narrow strip of mirror in the middle. Dad's wardrobe had no narrow strip of mirror. Dad would just have to guess at how he looked. I don't know when mum's wardrobe disappeared but now there is only dad's wardrobe and dad doesn't have any of his stuff in it anymore. Dad has now moved into the box room into a single bed to make room for the grandchildren Natasha and Vassia who now share his and my mum's old room. Dad doesn't mind. He's all right in the box room. His requirements have diminished. He has just room for a cupboard in the box room but the clothes in there are mostly superfluous. There are pullovers he has been bought for Christmas that he has never unwrapped, as he only likes to wear the same thing every day. He must look at the items, the pullovers he has never unwrapped, as though they are alien objects, eggs from an alien world, an alien civilization, which he is unwilling to interfere with. I don't know what happened to mum's wardrobe. It must have broke, shattered somehow, because that was the only way that wardrobe was going out of the house. On its knees.

27.

Cha Cha Cha

After a time, my mum wanted more. She wanted cha cha cha. She went with my dad to Latin American dancing classes and they started with the cha cha cha. My mum had loved dancing as a young woman. My dad less so, though they had met in Manchester at a dance hall. The unspoken reality was that dad wasn't very good at it. We tried to get him to show us what went on at these classes and he did a few darts around the living room to *one two cha cha cha, one two cha cha cha*, moving as if in some strange hieratic ritual, his legs bent low and his eyes focused in concentration. That was, I suppose, the template for the dance, and I imagine he never got beyond it. My mum looked on with a mixture of melancholy and wry amusement. Her idea of evenings out dancing the samba or the tango was never going to materialise.

My dad's interest in music was minimal. At first we did not have a record player and only heard records at Joe and Peg's. When we got one, the first record was *Mantovani and his orchestra* and the second was *Herb Albert and the Band I heard in Tijuana*. After that, they bought an LP of great tenor arias, famous bits from Italian opera, and sometimes, on days we didn't for some mysterious reason have the telly on, they sat in the front room with the light off and the record player on. I would be in the living room playing football with a rolled-up sock. A few years later my brother picked up the same habit and sat with the light off listening to Leonard Cohen.

Vernon Park

Dad did shift work as a plastic tube extruder. When he worked nights and we were at home we had to be quiet because he was in bed during the morning. He normally surfaced early in the afternoon, coming down unshaven in his vest. He didn't have a car until I was about fourteen when he bought an old Ford Cortina C reg. Up until then he walked across Vernon Park and got a bus to Romily from Portwood. Vernon Park was an ornate park built on a hill with a variety of huge trees. It dissolved into Woodbank Park which was bigger with open spaces for football and cricket. We lived on Woodbank Avenue, so dad could have got to Portwood through the two parks but when he was walking in the dark he preferred to bypass Woodbank Park by taking Turncroft Lane and getting into Vernon Park next to the museum which had mostly butterflies behind glass but did have a single mummy's hand. Mum made dad sandwiches for his lunch every day. This, by the way, was the only time the word 'lunch' was ever used in our house. By the time dad had bought that Cortina he had stopped doing shift work. Maybe there was less work and no need to have a shift system, or maybe once you got beyond fifty they stopped requiring you to do shift work. I don't know. One time late in his working career as a plastic tube extruder dad was presented with a watch by the head of the firm. He was interviewed in the works news sheet. They asked him *what do you like doing in your spare time?* Dad said *watching cricket,* which was a strange answer. *Watching football* might have made some kind of sense, but cricket? I don't think dad understood the rules of cricket. I think he was just bemused by the idea of answering a question like that. It must have stumped him. I think any question that wasn't factual he considered to be a trick question. So he gave (I think without premeditation) a trick answer. Maybe he thought he had to give a quintessentially English game as the answer. Maybe it was the answer he had stored up for questions like that, like the false birthday answer.

Stuffed Peppers

As a foreigner, dad needed his bread. There was a special plate on which what was called *your dad's bread* was put. White bread with a burnt crust. Dad liked the crust burnt. He was a godsend at Barkers the baker where we picked up our order on Saturday. *And there's a nice burnt one for you*, said Mrs Barker. *I know your dad likes that.* Dad often ate separately from us because of the shift work. We didn't mind leaving him all the burnt bits

One Saturday when mum and dad came back from town – mum worked on Saturday afternoon and dad went to pick her up from the big co-op where she worked in the pharmacy – they had brought a separate dinner for themselves. We had the usual for Saturday evening: a boiled egg followed by salad with some ham or, if we were having fish, a choice of tinned salmon or tinned sardines in tomato sauce. Instead of the egg, my mum and dad had this other thing: stuffed peppers. We had never had peppers before, even out of a tin as these were, and the smell was something exotic. Again, as on so many other occasions, I was bemused as to why my mum and dad should want something different for themselves, something that wasn't what we were having. On some other occasions on Saturdays, salami was bought for my dad. Salami, like peppers, was also foreign. Even my mum wouldn't have it. What she had that nobody had was tripe, though this normally at lunch time during the week, alone, as though shamefully.

Frank Ifield

Frank Ifield was a pop star in the early 60s. He had, I think, a No 1 hit with 'I remember you' and two or three more top twenty hits before disappearing into relative obscurity. He also yodelled. As a baby and toddler I loved Frank Ifield. This I was told me by mum and dad, although I had no real recollection of him when I was older. Years later in the mid-Seventies when I was a young teenager my mum came running into the living room where I was doing my homework. It was 'The Frank Ifield Show' on the telly. I had to watch it because of the family story that I loved Frank Ifield. He sang 'Would you like to fly in my beautiful balloon?' which was what everyone was singing in those days. It was a song that gave hope to an importantly marketable tranche of a generation. Then he had Ted Rodgers the comic on as his special guest star and was in stitches at Ted's lame quips. It was a lamentable show and soon taken off the air. But what a betrayal of the family story it would have been to say I did not like Frank Ifield anymore, the equivalent of Lear's daughters rejecting the ageing king. I remember a similar incident with Uncle Joe and Auntie Peg. The family story was that I loved jaffa cakes, and when many years later jaffa cakes and marshmallows were on offer I had to choose the jaffa cakes, even though I now preferred marshmallows. I watched my sisters eating marshmallows as I was stuck with the jaffa cakes that fate had inexorably ordained for me, observed by the smiling Joe and Peg, the Zeus and Minerva of 87 Edward St.

31.

Is it worth learning to ride a bike?

My dad told me that when he was in the war (the Second World War) he was running away from the Nazis (or was it the Communists?) and with his friends they got hold of some bikes but one of them couldn't ride a bike and he ran behind them, but he couldn't keep up and fell behind and eventually he got caught by the Nazis (or the Communists) and killed. He used to tell me that story to convince me how important it was to learn to ride a bike, because I couldn't ride a bike. Still can't. Though it did worry me, that story. What if I found myself in that position. I was a good runner, but surely not good enough to outpace the Nazis (or Communists).

A few years ago I read Günter Grass's autobiography where he told a story about what happened to him in the war. He was a young Nazi soldier trapped in a house outside Berlin with some other German soldiers during the taking of Berlin by the Soviets at the end of the war. They found some bikes and after a brief discussion, they decided they would make a break for it on the bikes. But Günter Grass couldn't ride a bike (or was it that there weren't enough of them?), so the captain told him to cover them as they rode off. The young Günter Grass knew it was tantamount to a death sentence as they left him alone in the house with the Soviet army advancing. But as he watched his compatriots riding off over the brow of the hill, he saw them all, every one of them, shot down dead, picked off by a Soviet sniper. Grass panicked. He ran out of the back door of the house and ran and ran until he found a railway track, which he followed for miles and miles, until, remarkably, he met up with a company of his own army.

So I was none the wiser about whether riding a bike could save my life or not.

32.

My Dad the Protagonist

It is normal to see yourself as the protagonist of your own life. After all, you are the consciousness. Who else is going to be the main character of your life? And as a child when you look at the grown-ups, their story, a story in which you don't really participate, who is the protagonist if not your mum and dad? But neither my mum or my dad were natural protagonists. For their own reasons, neither was comfortable in public. My mum in particular was ill-at-ease. My dad was actually quite sociable when called upon, but he was foreign. And what driving narrative was he engaged in? Who was interested in the story he was living? A man with a factory job and a wife and four kids. His drama was all in the thick weave of back-story, dark hidden narrative. As a boy, my empathy was with him. Observing him from the other side of the room with other men, Uncle Joe and Uncle Danny say, I would follow the rise and fall of the alien conversation, listening for when he intervened to give his opinion on Harold Wilson or Enoch Powell or Georgie Best. I sensed that these were not really his subjects because my dad was foreign and the fluent opinions that people had did not feel instinctive to him. You felt when you watched him that his opinions on Harold Wilson were randomly made up. He said them to participate but he didn't actually have any feelings about Harold Wilson or Edward Heath at all. As a stateless person, my dad didn't get a vote in the election. What I realized later was that the opinions that Uncle Joe had or that Uncle Danny or anybody else had were so fluent because they weren't making them up; they were just relaying their understanding of things from *The Daily Mirror* or *The Daily Express* or the telly from *Till Death Us Do Part*, whereas my dad had a distance from those things. With my dad you felt he would go along with the business of having opinions if he had to, but frankly he didn't care one way or another. The business of opinions was irrelevant to him. His life was under the shadow of what he had lived and the preoccupations of Harold Wilson or Enoch Powell, although not trivial, were not a part of the personal material he was wrestling with.

33.

Writing

The mechanics of writing were alien to my dad. When he needed to write, to sign a form or pen a note to the school explaining that I had to go to the dentist, he spent a few moments flexing his wrist, as though revving up for action. It was more in the manner of an athletic feat that he was preparing. When he put pen to paper, he did so in little flicks across the page so that the letters were built up as a series of minims, little strokes at acute and obtuse angles to each other with no rounds or curves to soften what almost looked like cuneiform lettering.

When I was growing up and testing out a signature, something that the teacher told me had to be unique, something that no-one could imitate and something that somehow had to represent your personality in its essence, my main aim was to avoid the soft bellied rounds and curlicues of childish or feminine lettering. I tried to form an autograph that was all angles and daggers. No graphologist would mark me down as indecisive or as sentimental. I see now that I was imitating my dad's script.

34.

The Seventies' Photos

There are a set of weird photos of us all taken in the seventies. We all have weird haircuts. My dad's got big sideburns like James Onedin from the *Onedin Line*, all us children have too much hair. I wanted to have my hair cut shorter but my mum wouldn't let me uncover my ears for some reason. You didn't see many ears in those days. David had long hair anyway. He had the longest hair in my secondary school. He was notorious. In the photos the curtains are densely patterned, as is the settee and the wallpaper. The photos look like Matisse paintings, all on one plane, all surface with no depth, and our faces are part of that surface. We look like an eccentric family, a family of axe murderers. My face is just a set of assembled features with no coherence to them, no character. It is as if all the features had been wrongly assembled from a number of different faces. My face looks out at the camera or across the living room with its mass of ornaments and you have absolutely no idea what is going on inside that head. My face, like everybody else's face in those pictures, is just one of the decorative features in the wallpaper. It could almost be one of those magazine puzzles. *Find the faces hidden in the curtain patterns and soft furnishings. Answers at the back of the magazine.* The creatures in this set of seventies photos have about the same importance as the soft furnishings.

35.

Houses

We lived in Stockport for my childhood. At first, when I was very little, in Portwood next-door to Auntie Mollie who had a grocer's shop. I have little memory of it. It was an old terraced house with an outside toilet. Then we moved to Offerton, first to Earnshaw Ave where we only stayed about eighteen months, then to Woodbank Ave near the park. The house in Portwood was knocked down a few years later along with a whole swathe of the area including St Paul's church. Only our doctor's remained. Dad still goes there. People don't like changing their doctor's, even when they don't trust them. Houses in those days in such places didn't cost more than two or three thousand pounds. Most of the money went on food. On Woodbank Ave me and my brother shared a room (and a bed), my two little sisters were in bunkbeds in the box room and my mum and dad had a room. At the back was a garden with two apple trees, one eater and one cooker. Many of the apples had worms inside them. There was also a tiny pear tree that never yielded fruit. It was a great garden for me with a decent patch of grass that we ruined by having a bonfire on Bonfire Night once, my dad succumbing to pressure from my brother. It was waterlogged for six months of the year. With my ball I regularly broke the windows at the back, and then my mum said *what will your dad say?* Mum spent a lot of time saying this. Dad didn't say much. He didn't like DIY at the best of times. DIY took him ages. A simple paint job on the windowsill meaning we were a month with newspaper on the floor. What he did, though, was give vent to his infamous quick temper. As my mum used to say, understating it, *he can be quick*. But then, he was a foreigner, so you understood why.

36.

Other Boys' Dads

Other boys had dads, though you did not see much of them. It was mostly the mums you saw when you went round to your friend's house. The mums gave you pop or a posher boy's mum once gave us ginger beer from a ginger beer plant. In working-class families, dads were like dragons, kept away from the public eye. You suspected they might be somewhere in the house, in bed maybe. Or else they might be at work. Often you checked, just to be sure. *Where's your dad?* If he wasn't at work or in bed, the place where he'd be was *out*, which was a place like any other. Then sometimes you saw the dads: sitting at the edge of a table through a doorway having their dinner with gravy and meat at eleven o'clock in the morning, unshaven, unapproachable, a million miles away, just looking at the wall or the table-top. Dads were mostly frightening. And then you heard them say something and didn't know what it was all about. Something about things that did not concern you, things that went on in this other home, and this dad was making no effort to let you feel that you could be part of it. Sometimes there were words they used that you didn't know. I remember Christopher Hyland's dad say to his wife *and he was skreiking his eyes out* and a few minutes later when we were at a safe distance I said to Christopher Hyland, who was my best friend in primary school, *what does skreiking mean?* It meant crying. And I was sure that we had words in our house that no other families would understand. For a long time I was sure that the word *landing* as in the *upstairs landing* was a word that only we in our family used, it was a word we had invented for our private shameful family reasons, and if ever the need came up to use this word in public I said the *upstairs hall*, because I knew people would understand that. Until one day I heard somebody else use the word *landing* and the scales fell from my eyes. It was a word. Other boys' dads used their own words too and one of them even tore nude pictures out of the daily paper and pinned them up on the wall, and I felt sorry for that boy and his mum and I won't even mention his name now for fear of embarrassing him if ever he reads this, although this is many decades ago and it could be that the mum and the dad in question and even the boy are now dead.

37.

My Education

If dad had had his way, me and my brother would have learnt a trade. There would have been a plumber and an electrician in the family. As a heating engineer installing central heating, Uncle Joe had always done well. Foreign holidays; a car (at first a three-wheeler but then the full four wheels); home movies; that picture of the Blue Lady up on the living room wall. Things we could only dream of. That was because Joe had a trade. My mum insisted we stay on at school. After all, we were at a grammar school: St Bede's, where her brother Jack, who died in the early seventies, had once won a scholarship (that would have been in the 1930s), only to be unable to go as he had to go out to work to earn money for the family. I think my dad was mostly bemused by it. One time – I would have been thirteen – I got a bad report at the Parents-Teachers meeting for lots of messing around and what my mum chose to tell me was that my dad was very disappointed as he was very proud of me. This cut me to the quick and I started doing better after that. Later on, when I got good A level grades I remember coming home and I said *I got my A level results today* and my dad said *how did you do?* And I said *Good. I got all As and distinctions in the S Levels*, and he said *is that good?* and I said *yes* and he said *good* and went back to opening the tin of vegetable soup. It was probably the best response he could have given. And when I started work the question was always *do you have enough work?* And I would always say *yes, I don't want to kill myself with work* and he'd say *you never know when you might need the money*, though nowadays when I say *I don't want to kill myself by working too hard*, he says *you're right*.

Laughing in Greece

We went to Greece for my sister Helen's wedding to Dimitris. Peg and Joe came, Auntie Molly came, my cousin Chris came, and the Yugoslav contingent came too: Drago and his daughter Branislava, Maria my dad's sister and Milan his brother. This was in 1994. It was an emotional moment for my dad. It was the first time my dad had seen his sister since he left Dalmatia at the end of the Second World War. When he had left she had been sixteen; now she was sixty-two and had no teeth. There was a moment when for some reason which I cannot recall my dad started laughing. I had seen him laugh before but on a human scale. This was something else, something frightening even. It was like the laughter of the Bacchae. He could not control his laughter or the distortions that the laughter did to his face. There is a scene in Zola's *Thérèse Raquin* where one of the characters who has committed a murder starts painting portraits but he can only paint one face, the face of his murder victim. The character looks at his hand and realizes that his hand had a mind of its own, it no longer belongs to him. It is a classic motif of Gothic literature, the part of the body that will not obey its master. This was how it was with my dad. The mouth was twisted out of all recognition and when I looked into his face I did not know who this person was.

39.

Behind the Settee

Like many children I spent a lot of time behind the settee. There was just enough room there for a nine-year-old. One day I was behind the settee and I heard my mum and dad talking about money. My mum was saying she didn't have enough of it. What with the shopping, the insurance man, the milkman, the window-cleaner, the coal-man, the laundrette, the pools-man, the children's dinner-money. My dad's jacket was on the back of a chair. Later when they had gone out into the kitchen, I went into my dad's inside jacket pocket and took out the five-pound note that was there. I found my mum's purse which was in her handbag and slipped the five-pound note in. A couple of hours later I heard the commotion from my place at the back of the settee. My dad was missing a five-pound note. My mum found an extra note in her purse. I had to admit I had made the transfer. My mum and dad looked at each other as you would say philosophically. My mum would have quietly explained why I shouldn't have made the exchange from pocket to purse. This must have shown where my loyalties lay at that age. Dad went out to work and came back for his dinner or his bed; he was half an outsider, a wolf of the steppes, while my mum was with us at home, the still centre of the world.

40.

Five Boys

I don't know why or how it came to pass but one day I found myself in Booth's, the local newsagents and sweet shop, with my dad. What he was doing there with me I don't know. There were places where he didn't tend to go. Down Graham Road to Booth's, for example. This was a short hop away from home and entailed crossing no roads. Even as a seven-year-old I was sent down there for sweets (my mum liked chocolate dragees or sugared almonds of Victory V lozenges; my dad would be bought anything with nuts in it; I don't know why the story of him particularly liking nuts emerged. I suspect he liked the idea of liking nuts rather than the nuts themselves. A Cadbury's *whole nut* bar might be what he got if he was at home and not on a shift). I also did the grocery shopping down Graham Road. I remember one day the usual grocer's shop was closed and a new shop had opened up next door called *Spar*. I looked through the window at people with metallic baskets (customers I thought) walking round the space handling items themselves and placing them in their basket independently of the shopkeeper. I had never seen a self-service supermarket before. I ran back home, not daring to go in. It was as if I had woken up into a new world where everyone knew new rules and I didn't. But on this occasion I was in Booth's with my dad, just me and him and I asked if he could buy me some chocolate. He chose the chocolate for me, which was unusual and made the event grander than if I had chosen my own chocolate bar. He bought me a brand called *Five Boys* chocolate, which was a strip of milk chocolate with the heads of five boys with different expressions gavelled into the chocolate. I think it was made by Fry's. I had never seen one of these bars before. It was a difficult decision to find a favourite amongst the five boys and eat him last. I don't know what happened to *Five Boys* chocolate bars. I don't know if I ever saw one again. In my mind it is associated with my dad. Maybe it hints at a narrative strain he had within him that we didn't see very much (why else choose an unknown bar with illustrative and fictional glamour rather than a better-known brand?). His choice of the *Five Boys* chocolate bar was a hint of a secret life that was seldom revealed.

41.

Letting Go

When I was studying for my A levels the teachers said I needed to go abroad to France or Germany in the summer to practice my languages. This was easier said than done. I had never been abroad. Unlike Peg and Joe we didn't have money for those kinds of holidays, so I would have to do it on my own. I found an advert for a so-called Youth Work Camp in *Baden-Würtenberg* in South Germany and applied for that. You had to be between 18 and 30 and I was seventeen, so I lied about my age. You were not paid for working (we were to build a children's playground or *Kinderspielplatz* in a little town called *Oberrot*) but had board and food paid for. I applied and was accepted. Somehow, I got money for the train and boat there, but didn't have enough for a return ticket. My brother had already started travelling in Europe and elsewhere by then and he hitch-hiked, so I thought I'd do the same to get back. It sounded straightforward. You stuck your thumb up and someone gave you a lift. And that was what happened. I spent four rather miserable weeks in *Oberrot* with grown-up young men and women in their twenties, all of us sharing a school hall with camping beds spaced out round the edge of the communal space, and then hitched home, sleeping the first night in a doorway in a North German mining town and the second night in a graveyard in Dover. I had just enough money for the ferry and a bus from Manchester to Stockport.

What astonishes me now is how and why my mum and dad let me go. Maybe I lied to them about having a ticket for the return journey. Maybe they thought I was being paid for the work and so would get some money for the ticket home. Maybe they were incredibly liberal and thought it would be good for me. Maybe they just thought that a seventeen-year-old was the same as a twenty-two or twenty-three-year-old like my brother. Maybe they went through a moment of obliviousness or bad parenting. Maybe they were just letting me go already.

42.

Being Foreign

It was different being foreign in the past, especially in the provinces. You didn't see foreigners. News would get round if there was one. People would nudge strangers and whisper quietly in their ear or just mouth the word surreptitiously, the F... word. In my primary school there were no first-generation foreign children and none in my secondary school either. Just a few second-generation foreigners like me, an Italian or two, a Pole or two, lots of Irish. That was in the seventies. In the fifties it would be even rarer. Nowadays, one way or another, everyone is foreign. But my dad would have got used to the idea of his exceptionalism.

I remember when he and mum came to visit me in Paris in what would have been the late eighties. We went in a cafe near the *canal St Martin* and my dad overheard people speaking Serbo-Croat. He was slightly bemused to hear this old language of his being spoken. He had so got used to it just lying dormant in a forgotten drawer in his mind somewhere. He approached one of the young men and had a brief exchange with him, but they were not particularly interested in speaking to my dad. It was their language; there were thousands of Serbo-Croat speakers in Paris, mostly of a younger generation, economic migrants, not political like my dad. Why would they want to speak to this ageing guy with halting syntax, stuttering through his forgotten language? I remember looking at my dad's puzzled and disappointed face. For him it would be an event to find a speaker of his mother tongue. To them, it meant nothing. He was probably thinking that the one thing he had been all these years – a foreigner - was an irrelevance here in a multi-cultural metropolis, and of course now it's an irrelevance everywhere. It doesn't matter that he's foreign anymore.

43.

The so-called facts of life

One evening when I was sitting in front of the telly with my mum watching a comedian the term *having it off* came up. In those days – this would be the seventies – comedy was very much the business of this kind of furtive sexual reference. *Having it off; having it away; a bit of skirt; some crumpet; getting your end away.* Nowadays these terms are mostly part of the past. But in those days they were what popular culture was and even a person as modest and demure as my mum could not fail to be contaminated by them. Anyway, my mum turned stiffly towards me and said *you know what that means, don't you?* I would have been about thirteen at the time. Without taking my eyes off the television screen I said yes. A few days later my dad came into the bathroom when I was having a bath. We have never had a lock on the bathroom door and whenever I said we should – they had locks on bathroom doors on the telly - I was laughed out of court as though my suggestion was the most risible thing anyone had ever heard. My dad hadn't been in the bathroom when I was having a bath for a few years, so when the door creaked open and he came in I feared the worst. First things first was to situate the islands of foam above my privates. I knew at once he was going to try and tell me the so-called facts of life, facts I had heard in various versions, official and unofficial, since the age of nine, starting at St Joseph's junior school when it got out that I didn't know what that term *having it away* meant. Bernard Shaw, the cleverest boy in my class, was called in to explain. The way he told it, I recall, was that a seed, like a grape seed rolled down the man's willy into the woman, and that seed was a baby which then grew inside the woman. When my dad started winding up towards that general direction, using I think the expression *it's time you learned what these things are for*, I told him in no uncertain terms that I knew about all that because we'd done it at school in Biology. Dad was relieved and, though he tentatively tried to broach the issue again from another angle, was ultimately happy to retire from the bathroom without having to go into any detail.

My mum would have got onto him and told him to have a talk with me. In fact, a few days after, she checked with me. *Did your dad have a talk with you the other day?* I again said yes without taking my eyes off the television screen. The real story here is not how the embarrassing story of the so-called facts of life was never quite imparted to me, but rather how my mum had to make sure my dad did what a dad has to do. She wasn't really checking on me; she was checking on him

44.

The Sporting Life

I never saw my dad run. Maybe grown-ups ran less in the past. They outgrew running quicker. Maybe my dad felt he'd run enough and was going to take things at his own pace, which is what he always did. For *at his own pace* read *slow*. One time I went with him to Woodbank Park along with a boy called Robert who lived two doors up from us and was my age. He didn't go to my school, so I didn't know him very well. My friends were school friends. As a child, I didn't invest in the neighbourhood. So we went to Woodbank Park and dad decided he'd give us a football lesson. Maybe he was thinking I'd be a professional footballer one day (I certainly did). The coaching session was all about trapping the ball. It seemed a boring skill to me, but dad put us through our paces and told us that you can't use the ball unless you can control it first and for that you had to trap it. I don't remember any other coaching sessions he put me through. Maybe he got fed up of the idea after that or maybe he only had stuff to say about trapping. I know Robert wasn't very taken with it. He was one of those boys who didn't like football but liked trucks and army stuff instead. He always wanted to play at being in the American army, which must have been a fantasy of his. Robert wanted us to play at him being an American soldier and me being the Viet-Kong, which seemed like a daft game to me as we were just pretending to shoot each other and die and then we could just make it up if we were only injured in the arm, as often happened on the telly. The other sport that my dad tried to get me involved in was swimming. He liked swimming, but I never took to it. Once at Primary school he came back from a parent-teacher meeting and said the teacher had said I was the model pupil. I did everything: writing; sums; talking; running; football. There was just one thing I couldn't get the hang of and that was swimming. That must have been a nuisance for my dad because swimming was one of the things he did. He continued to swim at the local pool till he was into his eighties, until gradually he started to complain of the cold and did it less and less until he stopped altogether.

45.

Aesthetic Positions

My dad didn't often have points of view on aesthetic matters. His main position on films on the telly was that they were good if they had a lot of *action* in them, by which he meant fighting, and he didn't like morally ambiguous characters but thought goodies and baddies should be clearly delineated. I remember once after an edition of *Are you being Served?*, the camp seventies BBC sit-com set in a department store, he said: *The man who wrote that must have been a really clever man*, and we all turned round and looked at him in horror. As I recall, it was a programme about a prediction or joke prophecy of some kind and the one detail I remember is that it was foretold that such and such a character would find themselves wearing a new hat, which was taken to mean that they would get a promotion, whereas in fact what happened at the end of the programme was that the character, whilst arranging stock in the stock room of the department store, had a box topple over onto him or her and a hat fell fortuitously onto his or her head, thus fulfilling the prophecy literally if not metaphorically. Anyway, dad thought this was a clever idea and we didn't.

Another time we were, for some mysterious reason, watching a programme about Picasso with David Hockney as presenter and Picasso's ability to draw hands was being highlighted and my dad said that, *in fact, Picasso wasn't as bad as everyone said.* Who this everyone was wasn't clear. Dad said the same thing another time when he was commenting on some glam rock band in the seventies, saying that *everyone said the Beatles were bad but they weren't as bad as this lot*, 'Sweet' or whoever they were, to which my mum said *no, everyone didn't say the Beatles were bad, just him* and we all laughed. What he most detested were talking culture programmes like *The Culture Show* where a panel of critics sit around and analyse the cultural offerings of the week. These people, especially if they were women, really got his goat and he could not repress his distaste of them. I never dared to tell him that all my years of fancy university training had equipped me for nothing other than such a role, that of someone who insisted on shooting his mouth off about stuff that didn't matter, just like those people on *The Culture Show*. The only thing I had going for me was that I wasn't a woman. Of course, my dad would never make the connection between anything I might do a few years later, an article in a broadsheet or a comment piece in the arts section of a high-brow weekly magazine, and what Germaine Greer was doing on the telly.

This was all conventionally reactionary. If ever we got a newspaper it was *The Daily Express,* which was a tabloid masquerading as a broadsheet, and at work he would have been exposed to the real tabloids. As was the case for many working-class men, liberal comment annoyed him, though he didn't mind it in the family, in private, as though what he really didn't like was people making an exhibition of themselves.

Ironically, my dad, with all the cultural and historical slings and arrows that had hit him in his life, should have been the person best placed to pursue cultural commentary. He was the accidental point of intersection for all the pressures that culture brings to bear.

My Dad's English

My dad's English was pretty good, considering. He had a good way with words. There were things he got wrong. We joked always about his use of the definite article. He stuck it in willy-nilly, coming out with phrases like *what are you the doing?* or *he is the no good or do you the know.* In fact, he probably only did this once in a while but we kept it in our imitations of him over the years. The way we characterised it was with my dad telling some roundabout story and my mum listening patiently before flattening it with some caustic epilogue. *Do you know what I the had today?* says dad. *What?* we say. *I had the something I never had before,* he says, building the tension. *What was that, dad?* we say. He looks earnestly at us as though about to utter some precious truth. *Shall I the surprise you?* he says again. *What was it?* we say again. *Hot toast,* he says. *What?* we say. *Hot toast,* he repeats. We are confused. *What do you mean, hot toast? We always have hot toast? No,* he says. *Really hot. Hot buttered toast.* Mum is listening from the kitchen where she is washing pots. She can bear it no longer. She comes in and takes control. *Get away with you,* she says. *You're the only one who never has hot toast. You're so slow to get it buttered. We all know what hot toast is, lad.* She calls him lad. Dad shakes his head while we all laugh.

When he is angry he swears under his breath but words come out, words like *blackguard* or is it *blaggard.* I don't know where he has got these words from? They are probably words he picked up somewhere before I was born, because this is what I forget, he has more history with the English language than I have. When you learn a language from scratch as a grown-up and have to survive in an alien community with such meagre tools, your experience of it must be so intense. Your learning is deep, deeper in many ways than the native speaker.

When we were little he used terms of affection that seemed

to us to be mostly taken from his dinner plate, words like *chop* or *cabbage*, as in *come over here, chop?* or *what are you doing there, cabbage?* I have never heard anyone else use these endearments. I don't know if he made them up or maybe translated them from his mother tongue.

47.

What you are and what you once were

Sometimes, after Communism was over, after 1989 or 1990 or 1991, we said to dad *why don't you go back to see you family. It's not Tito anymore. No-one will arrest you.* Dad had always said he couldn't go back to Yugoslavia because they wouldn't let him in and on his British Travel document it specified the one place he could not go to was Yugoslavia. But after the fall of Communism, that was over. The family had moved from Dalmatia to Belgrade now. We said *why not go and see everybody there?* Dad looked at us as if we were mad and as if this would be a betrayal of the life he had built up in England. He knew instinctively that there could not be two lives, there could only be one life. *The Soldier's Tale* by Stravinsky and Ramuz, based on a Russian folk tale, tells the story of a soldier who comes back from the war and spends three days enjoying the hospitality of an old man on his way home. Whilst staying with the old man he accepts to sell him his violin. When he gets back to his village, three years, not three days, have passed and his fiancée is married to another man. The soldier goes off in despair and comes to another kingdom where he learns that the daughter of the king is ill. She can't move or speak. The soldier wins back his violin from the old man who is, of course, the devil and cures the princess with the music from his instrument. In this way he wins her hand in marriage. And all should end happily ever after, but the soldier wants to go back to his old village with his bride to present her to his mother. When he crosses the boundary of the village he loses everything. The Princess is left behind and the devil has won. As the narrator says *You cannot be what you are and what you once were. You must choose between.*

48.

Dad's Wrist

There is a snapshot in my mind of my dad's wrist, the cuff of his shirt, the edge of his jacket and a wrist-watch with a metal strap. The jacket is some kind of sports jacket with hound's tooth check; the shirt is a type of long-sleeved cotton top. In my mind's eye he wore these things in the late sixties. All I have in my memory is the three or four-inch segment of wrist area like a frame on a spool of film. I realize that since fixing this recollection in my mind I have tried unconsciously to emulate it in myself, with long-sleeved cotton tops and a hound's tooth check jacket. I even once got a metal strap for my watch before realizing how uncomfortable it was, snagging on the hairs on my arm. More recently, since he has got older and since fashion moved to trick everybody into dressing badly in so-called sportswear, dad has dressed in beige a lot. If I go shopping with him now for something new he just looks for identical replacements for the article of clothing that has just definitively disintegrated, which is the reason for our visit to the *Marks and Spencer's* outlet store in Crown Point North shopping centre. If the match is not identical he is unhappy, the replacement is not as good. If I say *but these trousers are better*, he looks at me as if I am mad and says *how can they be better?* I remember once when I was showing him some photographs of something and he said *why don't you have them in the proper size?* To him the proper size was the small format that we had always had our holiday snaps in when we came back from Blackpool or Colwyn Bay or Llandudno or, once, from Scarborough. *These are bigger,* I said. *They're better. You can see the picture better.* He snarled back, unconvinced.

49.

Things my dad didn't know

I think at the end of the fifties or the beginning of the sixties my dad went to Paris. He met his brother Milan there. There is one photograph of that event. They are standing together staring at each other in an almost confrontational way though embracing each other at arm's length, observing each other almost, from close distance. The image is also at an angle as though the camera had been tipped intentionally by some artful photographer. Whereas, in fact, it would just have been some passer-by in the street in Paris who had taken the picture when asked by an anonymous pair of men and had toppled in taking it, to produce, fortuitously, felicitously, the raked image. When I asked my dad about his visit to Paris to meet his brother Milan he knew NOTHING about it, where he stayed, how he got there, what he saw there, what they did together, he and his brother. He had forgotten. I was sometimes alarmed by what my dad had forgotten, what he didn't know. Once, when we were watching something on the telly, the word *blues* came up, as in *blues music*, and he said *what's that?* I was shocked that he had lived for seventy years as it was at the time, forty-five or so in England and didn't know what the word blues meant. Had he never been curious to know what this word meant that he must have heard a thousand times? And how many other basic units of knowledge had bypassed him? To what extent was he wandering around in a mist. There were lots of things he just didn't know. To what extent had dad always been like olde dad, wandering around lost?

50.

Hitting Me

Sometime my dad hit me. I don't blame him. I don't think he hit the girls and if he hit David it was before my time. But he hit me sometimes. He lost his temper and he chased me. I scampered away. Upstairs; under the bed; out into the back. I was a pest. I did some pretty rotten stuff. I remember – I can't think why I did this. What was I up to? - I used to wipe my bottom on the bathroom towel. I was warned about it and I did it again. I remember the moment when I thought about doing it, and I went and did it, leaving brown skid marks on the bathroom towel. It was just the last of the wiping that I did on the bathroom towel, just the final flourish. There was no thought of the consequences. To my mum and dad it would be incomprehensible. No wonder my dad got furious. What was going through my head? I didn't really bother that he hit me or chased me around. It was fair do's. It was life, when I was ten or twelve or thirteen, or whatever I was. One time my mum gave me a £5 note for some shopping and I lost it. My dad took years to get over that. How could I lose a £5 note? £5 was a lot of money in those days. Another time I broke the light shade in the living room with a tennis racket that I was playing with. My dad was out. Mum told him that it had just fallen down, spontaneously. He believed her. Years later she told him I'd broken it. By then it was too late to chase me under the bed. I was eighteen and wasn't wiping my bottom on the bathroom towel any more.

A Little Death

Dad was mostly well. I only ever remember one problem he had, which was kidney stones and him going to hospital for a couple of days to have them out. It was because he had too much salt on his dinner, mum said. Later, he went to hospital another time to have his varicose veins done. And when he was older, just after mum died, he had both his eyes done for the cataracts. I remember taking a photo of him on a very hot day in Joe and Peg's back garden, sitting there with shades on and a green tarpaulin background for some reason.

When he was still at work, not long before he retired, I remember mum telling me how one day he had suddenly had a fit and fallen down unconscious. She was sure he was dead and went down on her knees to see. She said she thought he was dead for a few seconds, but then suddenly, he came back to life. He was fine. I don't think they even sent for the ambulance or the doctor. Nothing like that had ever happened to him before and nothing like that ever happened again. It was just an aberration, or maybe a reprieve, a little semblance of a death, a small manifestation of the possibility, its imminence at all times, its omnipresence, a slight flexing of its muscle.

We are dying slowly all along. All our options are disappearing, one by one, as we move through life. In the end, when we are very old, all the options have run out: the physical; the mental; the human. And at that moment, the idea might be, you embrace death. That's the idea anyway.

My mum had an idea that dad would outlive her. He was strong and healthy and she had a history of sickness. She did the thinking for him on this and tried to prepare him for when she was gone. Dad listened obediently when she tried to tell him that he needed to think about that, but he wasn't happy thinking about it. He wasn't very reflective.

He never liked thinking about unhappy eventualities. Maybe the little death made him think that he'd go first, but he didn't, she did. The little death just re-centred him, gathered him together for lots more life.

52.

Molly's Parties

Auntie Molly, who was the eldest of the siblings on my mum's side of the family, used to have a party every few months. They lived in Cheadle which is quite a rich area in what was termed a big house. They had always had shops and must have made money. Molly's husband was Danny or Danny Neal as people said. They had two sons, Terence and Young Danny. That was the way of it. Uncle Joe's son was also called Joe, Young Joe. We still call him Young Joe though he must be getting on towards seventy now. Anyway, the Neal's were a musical family and in these parties there was always a bit where they sang round the piano, *Danny Boy*, and songs like that. For us, this was excruciating. Then Young Danny would get his bagpipes down and do a bit of that. People had been getting mildly pissed and dropping bits of tinned tangerines down various cleavages. That was probably the limit of the debauchery. My dad kept pretty much apart. Sometimes he was involved in a political discussion with the men: Danny, Young Danny, Danny's brother Bill Neal, Uncle Joe, Young Joe. As a boy I remember thinking how I wished I knew about politics to be able to participate. And then a few years later when I listened in, I saw that it wasn't really a discussion, just an airing of grievances and prejudices.

One time when I was little I remember saying I wanted to spend the night away from home (I must have seen things on the telly where kids are away from home and have adventures) and Uncle Danny came for me in the car and whisked me away to Cheadle. They had savoy cabbage and Sirloin with very dark gravy for tea, and after a few questions round the dinner table they got on with talking about their stuff and I was pretty much ignored. It was a household where children were not the centre of attention. The next day dad turned up quite early to take me home on the bus. I suspect mum and dad were worried about how I would be getting on with Molly who, as my mum used to say, could be sharp.

53.

In the Pub

My dad was never a great pub-goer. When I was little he tended to go before Sunday dinner. We had Sunday dinner about five o'clock because we had had a late egg and bacon. So dad went to the pub on his own and had maybe two pints of bitter. When I was old enough to go to the pub with him when dad was living in Denton, I always wanted to go to what my sister called the old man's pub because I liked the beer there. My dad didn't like the old man's pub. Firstly, because it was more old-fashioned, maybe rougher. Secondly, because the beer was marginally more expensive. I suspect this latter reason was more pertinent. Money was the persistent demon nagging always at the back of his mind and he would feign a preference in a beer because he knew it was threepence cheaper. Later, he started drinking Guinness in the winter and, when he started having what he called a funny taste in his mouth, he switched to mild, though I suspect he had also noticed that mild was a few pence cheaper.

In the pub the issue of conversation looms large. There is no telly, nobody else around to dissipate the dialogue, you have to talk. So we do the weather; we do other family members; we used to do Man Utd but he has drifted out of touch with this; we do the beer, what there is now and what there used to be; we always mention *Wilson's* bitter and the change that came over *Boddington's* which in Manchester is seen as like the date of the Great Schism and I always say how I like *Robinson's* because it reminded me of primary school. The school was built next to a *Robinson's* brewery and when the smells came out from the brewery we always thought it meant it was cornflake pie for lunch. So we normally manage a conversation, though it is alas the same conversation each time.

54.

Der Verschollene

Kafka's so-called America novel used to be called *America*. In recent years the scholars have renamed it *Der Verschollene* in German or *The Man who disappeared* or *The Man who went away* in the English translation. Most stories are about men who come back, not men who go away. Ulysses comes back. He's already away and he comes back. In *Der Verschollene*, Karl Rossmann, the protagonist, is sent abroad to America by his parents because he has got a maid in the family home pregnant. As he arrives in the port of New York he sees the Statue of Liberty with the figure of Liberty holding, in Kafka's world, a sword not a beacon above its head. Kafka never finishes the novel. It peters out, but the adventures that he did write tell of the hero going from one substitute family to another, which is I suppose realistic enough for a young man away from home for the first time. He goes from the harsh punishment of his father back home to his Uncle Jakob whom he meets on the ship to America to a maternal cook at the Hotel Occidental and on through a series of adventures in which he repeatedly tries to find his place and is forever harshly ousted.

When my dad left what was at the time Yugoslavia and the chaos of the end of the war, he went from camp to camp as a displaced person. As a very young man he would have had someone who looked out for him. When he finally arrived in Britain, at first in Wales near Swansea and then in Manchester, it would have been a solitary life, not speaking the language adequately, far away from everything he knew. Then he met my mum and the construction of another family began. I remember a few years ago he said to me that what he really wanted was for him and all of us children to live together in his house (what was his tiny house at the time, pre-extension). He didn't see how it might not appeal to my brother and me, two middle-aged men living in London, or my sister living her own life on the other side of Manchester with her daughter. His ideal was to have everything regress to how it had been decades ago, a mass of bodies shifting around in a tiny space and him sitting still at the centre.

55.

Mum's Death

Mum died suddenly. They were sitting in front of the telly. At this time they lived alone, just mum and dad, a retired couple. Mum collapsed onto her side on the settee. It was an aneurysm. It only lasted a couple of minutes. She must have suffocated. My dad was next to her, not knowing what to do. She pressed his hand. Dad phoned 999 but she was dead when the ambulance came. He would have tried ways to revive her, ways he might have seen on the telly on hospital dramas or police dramas when the cop's buddy is laid low. My mum always used to say she hoped he'd go (die) before her as he wouldn't know how to cope. I didn't listen to this particularly, but she was right. He hasn't known how to cope. She had been the engine of the couple. After the death he turned his anxieties to fretting about the funeral costs. It was a pragmatic thing he could fix his mind on. When mum was laid out in the funeral parlour we got the chance to go and see her for the last time. I said I didn't want to go. Dad said I should go. I said I didn't want to. The church was nearly empty for the funeral. Mum and dad had never really done friends and much of the family was dead. How can you go through life, happy, charming, generous and then have nobody around at your funeral? After the funeral when I was in the car about to be ferried back to the station I waved to dad in the doorway. He was there, diminished. He was back on his own again, like all those years ago when he had left Dalmatia.

56.

An Insect Jig

My dad had this little tune, not so much a tune, more a little insect jig rhythm, that he would whistle. You suspected it was a Balkan rhythm, something he had brought back. Although it could equally have been his adaptation of some Western pop song into a Balkan mode. If we asked him what it was, he said he didn't know. Dad brought nothing back with him from Dalmatia, nothing in his head that he ever cared to share at least. No memories of food or drink; no songs or stories. The only joke I ever heard him tell was of a man who couldn't put his trousers on. I remember him miming a man trying to *jump* into a pair of trousers. I don't know what the punch line was. Maybe it was just the image of the man and the empty trousers that tickled him. We were immune to the joke (whatever it was) but tickled by dad's jumping motion and his delight at the image.

When we asked him what he had wanted to be when he was growing up, he said a farmer, which we couldn't understand. Not that we thought he might want to be a footballer or an astronaut, but maybe an engine-driver or a doctor. He didn't know anybody who didn't work on the land, so wanting to be an engine-driver was probably like wanting to be the King of Timbuktoo. When you pushed him to explore his deepest, most impossible desire, it would be owning seven goats or something like that. Aged eight or nine, that really did NOT get my juices going.

57.

The man who went away

Seen from the other angle, from the angle of the people that were left behind, the brother, the sister, the pregnant wife, the mother, the father, they would not know at first that this was a definitive escape. It might have seemed to them at first a temporary disaffection. Then a new political reality sets in. There is work to be done. There is no news. The world is in chaos. Millions are displaced in Europe. Boundaries are redrawn; alliances are reforged. Years pass. They get used to it. And then, so much time has passed that it seems all to be like another world, now passed, childhood, now outgrown. My dad's dad, whom I saw in one photo which must have dated from the 1950s for Drago is a boy next to him, was a tall man with a big moustache. My dad has told us that people used to call him the American, because he had been to America. But he came back. Maybe that was the feeling about my dad. He had gone away. But he would come back one day, like his dad before him had come back from America. Like Ulysses who came back to Ithaca. Like many heroes of stories who come back, often wiser, sometimes broken. But time went by and my dad did not come back. And, many years after, in a few little sorties by Drago, by Drago's daughter Branislava, who came to England, by our cousin Nada (Maria, dad's sister's daughter), who came to visit me in Paris and came to stay for a time in London, by Mumchala, another cousin (Milan's son), who also came to visit, speeding through Paris one morning, turning up at my little flat on the isle St Louis and insisting on drinking slivović for breakfast, they came to us, emissaries, if you like, or heralds or scouts sent on in advance to test the terrain. Until there was the final engagement in Greece when my sister got married on neutral territory, where (who knows?) things may have been spoken, though in a language that I could not follow.

It turned out, then, that from their perspective, looking back now in hindsight by those that still remain there, those that have not died in the long interim, that he definitively was the man who went away.

58.

A Proper Watch

One day, after mum had died and dad was living with Helen and Dimitris and their two girls Natasha and Vassia in the house in Denton, probably before the extension had been put in, Helen told me that a man had approached dad near Crown Point North Shopping Centre. Dad had told Helen this story. He'd said *a man came up to me and he said Hallo How are you doing? And he said I remember you. How good you'd been to me a few years back. Do you remember?* And dad hadn't quite remembered but the man was very sure about it and he said *How are you?* And they'd shaken hands, had a bit of a chat and the man had said *Hey I tell you what, it's good I've bumped into you like this 'cause I've got these watches. Cracking watches they are. Have a look at this!* And he'd showed dad these beautiful watches. And he said *listen, don't tell anybody but why don't you have one for £50.* And they were beautiful watches and the man said, Oh how nice dad had been to him and his wife those years ago and dad couldn't quite remember but it must have been true. And anyway they were beautiful watches and dad said he didn't have £50 on him and the man said *well, what have you got?* And dad only had £28 on him and the man said *don't tell anybody, will you?* and he let him have it for £28. And when dad came home he was smiling and he said to Helen *do you know what I've the got?* And he showed Helen the watch, which, for Helen was just a cheap watch you could get off Denton Market for £5 these days, though dad was having none of that and he said *what the scrap are you the saying? It's damn good watch. It's proper watch.* And Helen said *they're all proper watches, dad. You mustn't be taken in like that by people you meet on the street* and dad said *Scrap. What are you the talking about?* But afterwards he didn't talk much about that watch.

Sensory Deprivation

Dad was depressed after mum died. He didn't want to change anything. He would go on watching the soaps that mum had wanted to watch, even though they did not interest him. This was by way of homage. Nothing changed in the décor. All the ornaments that had been around in my youth were still there stacked along surfaces, too many for the surfaces, all jostling for position in a sorry faded pageant, so that sometimes there was one ornament in front of another, all gathering dust: mostly animals in porcelain or glass or wood, or old mini football trophies I had won with the school team in the seventies, stuff that should have been turfed out years ago. The bedroom stayed the same with the pictures my mum had put up, impressionist prints by Renoir, or a souvenir of Paris balanced for equity's sake by a souvenir from Greece and a photo from Afghanistan David had taken on a trip there and something from Liz, so that all the kids got a look in on the parental bedroom wall. And dad would continue to sleep on his side of the bed while my mum's side lay vacant, as though awaiting her return. On her side of the bed was a little photo of Florie her mum as she had been near the end and a black and white picture of her dad in First World War army uniform. Where were the pictures of dad's family on his side of the bed? There were none. But neither were there souvenirs, trinkets, *objets* that attested to his own personal understanding and appreciation of the past. In fact, all his tastes and any keys to his identity were just the mirror images of my mum's personality that she had smuggled through for him. His past was a blank. And now dad just switched off most of his circuits, ran down the machine, engaged in sensory deprivation, running on the emergency current, no taste for things, no appetite, a retreat ever closer into a tiny core, until there was hardly anything there:

conversations about weather; the maintenance of a strict routine whereby decisions and new thoughts need not be touched on. But maybe that was what dad had always been like anyway and we'd just never noticed. Without mum to put stuff in the machine there was nothing going through and the mechanism was just turning round and round uselessly, performing hopelessly, pointlessly.

60.

Killing a Fly

I killed a fly. It was getting on my nerves. You butter the bread; put it on the table; the fly's on the bread. It keeps fizzing at you like a mosquito. Flies spread germs. Don't they? So I killed it, got it over by the window with Natasha's A level copy of *Huis Clos* and flattened it. After I killed it, olde dad – olde dad who once threw his daughter's present to him into the bin in front of her eight-year-old eyes; olde dad who had the least empathy of anyone I ever knew – that olde dad got all bleeding heart on me. *Big man*, he said and then *Man with a gun*. He delivered these two judgements with expert deadpan sarcasm. I couldn't believe it. Where did he get this empathy for a fly? Since when was he William Blake? Where did he get this wit? Since when was he George Orwell? So now I, as I make him his prunes and custard, as I chaperone him across the main road, as I administer his pills, as I jovially repeat the same conversation about the weather, his food or the time of day for the umpteenth time, I am the villain of the piece because I killed a fly. It reminds me of once when a man I knew, a banker, bought an artwork, and I asked him how much he had paid for it and he said to me that some people knew the price of everything and the value of nothing and I said *just a minute you're the banker*. By refusing to mention figures, you are the one sanctifying money. Whatever. What am I supposed to do? Usher the fly out the backdoor? I'm happy to do that for a daddy-longlegs or a spider but with a fly you're on a hiding to nothing. A fly would lead me as merry a dance as olde dad has been doing for months now. No, olde dad, I draw the line at flies.

61.

The man who slowly erased himself

I sometimes wonder if I will follow the same spiral that my dad has followed. That paring down process, the purification to the bone that has been happening in recent years. Biologically, you have to say, in the same way as I have his back, or his hair-line, or his lips, I surely will. I surely am doing so already. I can already feel myself shrinking into a tight core of preoccupations, appetites, responses. Of course, our nurture has been different. My nurture might push me somewhere else, but I doubt it. I actually feel I am starting to recreate the process that my dad went through. Here, imagine the mad scientist in the Hammer horror laboratory turning to his creature and uttering the words: *The process is recreating itself!*

There is a sense in dad that he piggybacked on mum much of the time, reading the books that she read, watching the telly she watched, going along with what she thought, what she did. In couples this always happens, but with dad it was extreme. When you took away what mum gave him, I'm not sure what was left. There were no articles, no things, no keepsakes of a former life. That dictionary got thrown out years ago. What was it that we found in dad's drawer? Nothing. Scraps of rubbish. He was a man who slowly erased himself. *Der Verschollene.* And to what extent do I reproduce this behaviour? When I feel whitewashed out of history, as can happen sometimes, I am unhappy about it. To what extent did dad want to leave no trace, to be that man who disappeared, I don't know. When I close my eyes and recreate his silhouette now, it is mostly a biscuit brown outline against the raspberry background. In time it will fade into the block of fizzing red and become just part of the wall.

62.

Peplums

When I was little dad used to take me to the pictures sometimes during the day. It must have been the weekend, or else in the school holidays. On a day when he was on the night shift maybe. We went in the afternoon and saw one of those Greek or Roman epics, peplums is the special word they have for them in French. *Demetrius and the Gladiators; The Seven Labours of Hercules. Ulysses and the Giants.* They were Italian films, I think, dubbed into English. I don't know why they were showing them at the picture houses in the afternoon when they should have been showing *Emmanuelle* or *Confessions of a Window-Cleaner.* My dad took me to see them, but I think he liked them mostly. Tales of fabulous strength with handsome heroes and exotic mythical exploits. We would go to the Essoldo in Mersey Square in the centre of Stockport or another cinema on Wellington Road just down from the library. I think it was called The Ritz. This was before the days of the ABC. My dad liked action films. Even now David says to him *Why don't you watch this film dad? It's a really good one.* He is referring to films like *Gladiator,* which would have interested my dad before. Now he is uninterested. Action films do little for him. Entertainment in general does little for him. He went through a phase of insisting on listening to the same cassette of Andrea Bocelli every night about 11.30. This was before we had the extension and, whatever was going on had to stop. At 11.30 he would say *I have to have my music on now,* and we all had to go to bed or sit and listen to it. I had no choice as I was sleeping downstairs. That was my cue for going upstairs and sitting on my dad's bed to read until he eventually tired even of Andrea Bocelli and fell asleep in the chair. Then I came downstairs and made myself some toast and waited till he went to bed. No, there are no peplums going on in olde dad's house these days.

63.

Irish Christian Radio Stations

In the last couple of years olde dad has taken to listening to the radio at night before he goes to bed. The days of Andrea Bocelli are over. He puts his electric blanket on and comes downstairs to put the radio on. He makes himself a glass of rum and blackcurrant, which he calls his poison. I don't know how he found the Irish Christian radio station but now the radio is fixed on that wavelength. The guy whose show it is at that time of night, who must be a Catholic priest, does a few minutes talk and then puts on a piece of music, usually an easy-listening Christian folk song sung by some Irish duo or trio, or else a lone Irish soprano with a thin, pure voice. When the presenter talks in his sing-song Irish way he says: *And people come to me, people come to me and they say father, when I go into the house of the Lord how must I dress and I say unto them, I say, it matters not how you dress in the house of the lord. Whether you come in fine clothes with a fancy cravat and fine leather shoes or whether you wear simple garb, the simplest of outfits, it matters not, for the Lord sees beyond your clothes, he sees into your hearts and knows what you are thinking, he knows what you are feeling. And he cares not what clothes you wear, for he does not judge a man by the externals but by his words and his deeds. So I say to you, go into the house of the Lord dressed however way you wish for the Lord sees into your very heart. And now here's Jake and Brian Macaffery singing of a very special vision that an old tinkerman had one night on the road from Limerick to Cork.*
I don't think olde dad knows what is being spoken, I'm not even sure he realizes it's religious but the rhythm is soothing and rockabye. We all go *Dad, can't we have something else on. There's a good film on Channel 4,* but dad won't have it. It might be that he falls asleep in his chair and we sneakily switch it off but the moment it goes off he knows something is wrong and wakes up. You'd think you could trick olde dad but it's not that easy.

64.

In the Ruins

I phoned my dad up for his birthday. The phone call is becoming an increasingly difficult procedure. Dad has never had much truck with phones. We got our first phone when I was in my twenties, so he never had the training. You can't let the silences linger in a phone conversation. I say *How are you doing?* Jovial is my manner. *No good,* says dad. I try and pick the tone up. *What are you up to?* I trill. He won't be up to anything. He doesn't respond to my joviality. He knows that I know he won't be up to anything and he's not going to go along with this subterfuge. I fall back on the ancient questions. *How's the weather?* Invariably cold, even in a heat wave. *What did you have for dinner?* He can't remember. *It was something,* he says. I pull a face on my end of the line. Ah! Something! *Have you heard from David?* I ask. He can't remember. *Have I seen David?* he asks. I say no. Me and David live in the same city but we don't see each other. We are a family that cultivates its silences. *No,* I say, *I haven't seen David.* Dad says *Ah!* as though this were an informative response. I ask him if he's been for a walk today. *Have you been up to Crown Point?* I say. Dad says he'd been to *Bargain Booze* to get some lemonade. He asks me what I've been up to. I say I've been out in the park. I say *how old are you now then?* He says *hundred and ten.* Hundred and ten is still a joke but not much of one. When you're in your nineties you should be saying hundred and fifty.

There are just stones here, dust and stones in this conversation. Maybe the outline of what was once a separate chamber. This was clearly once the nave; this was once the clerestory or the apse or the west aisle. Now it's just a couple of old stones in the grass. We can conjecture that once solemn rites were spoken here. Now there is traffic in the background. A new dual carriageway where the altar once was.

65.

Becoming a Marionette

In Kleist's essay *Uber das Marionettentheater* (1810) (About the Puppet Theatre) the author tells how Herr C. the director of ballet from the Opera is seen admiring the grace of the movements of marionettes at the local puppet theatre. Herr C. explains that the marionettes have no self-consciousness and in a sense they are free. It is man's self-consciousness that makes him unable to follow the forces of gravity with such grace and perfection. Man is born in an unfortunate position, caught between two worlds: the unselfconsciousness of the animal and inanimate world, on the one hand, and the infinite consciousness of a god. Man is a botched creature, a flawed prototype.

Of course, puppets are manipulated by an outer hand. In a sense, they have no freedom at all. The freedom that they have is the freedom of a Zen monk who aspires to the state where self-consciousness falls away and he becomes part of the natural world. We cannot become gods; maybe we can become marionettes.

Dad is becoming a marionette. He is not much part of this world now. He sits there and obeys the flow of the seasons, the routines of the family imposed by some puppet-makers from above. He sits and lets the sun play on his face. He is just part of the natural world. Sometimes he claps his hands together, to hear the sound, to feel his hands. And there are other brief sorties out of the world of the marionette, where he makes a twisted point, where he tricks us non-marionettes to reveal the absurd mechanisms of our constructed behaviour, but mostly now he lets the macrocosm flow over him. Old dad is becoming the marionette.

THREE

Olde Dad

I am sleeping on the living room floor at my olde dad's
again this Christmas. The house is full, so there is no
option but that's fine. I have an idea it's good for my back.
I fold the double quilt in two, sleep on one half and cover
myself with the other half. The house is heated like a
sauna. Eventually I get to sleep. Then my olde dad starts
his night-wanderings through the house. The first time he
comes into the living room is about two in the morning. I
have just dropped off. The light goes on with a loud clock
of the switch. I am stirring. He pushes me. *Are you all right?*
he says. I am now awake. *Yes. Why wouldn't I be all right?* The
light is directly above where I am sleeping on the floor.
Are you cold? he says. *No. It's boiling in this house. What did you
wake me up for?* He mutters and sits in his armchair above
me next to the full glare of the overhead light. I clench my
eyes and try and get back to sleep. After ten minutes the
light goes off. He's gone back upstairs. I am just getting to
sleep when he's down again. Clock! goes the heavy light
switch. I stir. *I need a drink*, he says. He's sits in the armchair
above me and I hear him do one small gulp of a glass
of water. Ten minutes later he's back up. This is now the
middle of the night. He's back down again an hour or so
later for a little walk round the living room. It's maybe four
in the morning. Clock! goes the light again. At six in the
morning the wall clock starts its hourly chimes. It is a novel
chime which has a different bird call on every hour. Six
o'clock is the barn owl, seven is the wren and eight is the
blackbird. Most instructive, but not necessarily what I'm
wanting after a sleepless night. But by eight my olde dad's
up again, this time definitively, sitting in his armchair in
his day clothes muttering information about the day. When
Helen comes down I hear him say; *he can sleep, that lad.* I
look up through red raw eyelids to where he is sitting above
me on his armchair like the *victor ludorum*. I've been in this
house twelve hours, I'm exhausted already. Why doesn't

olde dad put the glass of water in his bedroom? you ask. Clearly you know nothing of these things. The glass of water is his periscope. Through this feature he keeps some form of control: sleep deprivation in his counterparts; a panopticon over his domain. Olde dad will not renounce his power without a fight. You will have to wrestle the crown from his brow.

Samuel Beckett went through a period in his writing where he was obsessively interested in trying to exhaust permutations. *Watt* is the great deranged novel of this ilk. And then there is the scene in *Molloy* where the main character spends much time rearranging limited numbers of items in limited numbers of positions. In a famous scene he does this with pebbles (or are they coins?) into a set of pockets. My dad is like that. I am stretched out in the floor in sleeping position.

Dad: I'll switch the lights off

Me: Right dad.

Dad: I can't see to go through now.

Me: Put the hall light on.

Dad: I haven't locked the back door.

Me: Right dad.

Dad: I'll have to put the light on again.

Me: Right dad.

Dad: I need that hall light on again.

Me: Right dad.

Dad: I didn't take my pill.

Me: Right dad. What's it for?

Dad: Old people's things.

Me: Right dad.

Dad: I'll put the hall light on again.

Me: Right dad.

Dad: I can switch this light off now.

Me: Right dad. Remember to switch the hall light off when you go up.

Dad: Did I bolt the door?

Me: Don't know dad.

Dad: I'll put that light on.

And so on.

Martin Creed should live with my dad for a few nights. That'd sort him out.

68.

I am sitting on the sofa in the extension part of the living room trying to read and I can hear my brother talking with my olde dad in the living room proper. My brother says: *do you still take yourself to the barbers?* There is a silence while my olde dad tries to understand the question. I too try and understand the question. I shout out from my sofa: *What are you talking about? How else can he get his hair cut if he doesn't take his own head there! Nobody can take his head there for him, can they?*

My brother persists:

— Do you still go to the barbers in the market square?

— What market square?

— The market square next to Crown Point.

— I don't know where you mean.

— The square next to Crown Point where they used to have a market.

— What?

— In that square where they have a fountain next to Crown Point.

— Ah!

— Where they have a fountain.

— What?

— They have a fountain in that square.

— Do they?

— Do you still get your hair cut in that square near Crown Point where they have a fountain?

— No. I have hair cut in market square.

— That's what I was saying.

— No no, I go to market square to get hair cut.

— That's what I was saying.

— No I go to market.

My brother gives up. I return my eyes to my reading matter.

We are sitting watching Bony M on Top of the Pops 2. It is Christmas night entertainment. These are the big hits of 1978. My dad turns round and looks at the clock. *What time is it?* he says. *Eleven o'clock* we say. *Morning or night?* he asks after a moment's hesitation. *Look around. We're all around sitting watching the telly. The blinds are drawn. What do you think? I don't know,* he says, looking round. I can see his point. Here we are in 2014, watching a programme from 1978 with a confected simulacrum of a pop group singing about the exile of the Hebrews to Mesopotamia hundreds of years before Christ as though it were an update on a package holiday by a low-cost carrier. A few minutes later the same question. *Is it eleven at night or in the morning?* he says. *Night, dad. That's why it's dark outside,* we say. *It's dark in the morning too,* he says. He's right there and all. A few minutes later the same question. At this stage Abba are singing a happy song about being in love. 1978. That was all up the spout by then too. They were divorcing. Basically, my olde dad's main relationship now is with Time. They track each other; lose each other's scent; lay traps for each other. I thought there was something wrong when he was eating his cereals after Christmas dinner, which we have about five in the afternoon. I suspected then that Time had given him the slip. If he does not follow his strict regime of events in the day, mostly food events, he's adrift. Last night at half-one I was still trying to get him to go to bed so that I could sleep in the living room. He was still convinced it was the morning. He kept saying *I haven't done anything today. I just got up.* There is a passage in Proust where the narrator is astounded as to how each time we wake up from sleep we wake up with our own identity intact. It reassembles itself from the swirl of sleep in a sudden, miraculous adjustment every time we wake up. With my olde dad that miraculous reconstruction that should happen every time we wake up is starting to disintegrate.

Buying presents for my olde dad was never easy even when he was a younger dad. Once my sister made him a 'tool box' from a shoe box and crepe paper that she had seen on Blue Peter. He had thrown it out by Boxing Day. My mum made him get it out of the bin and parade it in front of my sister again, this time with gratitude. This act was alien to my olde dad even then. Now, forget it. On Boxing Day we were at my other sister's for dinner, and DVDs of the children when they were little were put on. I myself am hardly able to contain my boredom, but olde dad is completely uninhibited: He suddenly acquires a bad back (not even the bad shoulder!) and he has to be ferried home. Suits me. We got back in time for *Match of the Day*. Olde dad took a yellow card for the lads, as they say. This year I didn't bother. Got him some chocolates. Everybody else had taken the clothes options already anyway. Long-johns; woolly hats; jumpers galore; gloves; thermal socks. It makes no difference. Two years ago I bought him quite an expensive posh jumper from some fancy shop. I saw it was still in his cupboard unwrapped yesterday. And last year I got him some fur-lined leather gloves. They've vanished and he's back on the old acrylic £2.99 gloves he's always worn. So there's no point bothering. You learn to treat the whole business as ritual rather than real life. You repeat the lines laid out for you because new ones won't be heard anyway, and you worship the old objects once more on the altar of the olde dad. It's the only way. Bend unto it or be swept away! Resistance is futile.

This morning I was awoken by the carbon-copy of a conversation I had already participated in six months ago when I last stayed here, but this time it was my brother David playing my part. Olde dad says *I have to go to see doctor.* David says *what's wrong?* Olde dad says *I'm bad.* David says *where do you feel bad?* Olde dad says *everywhere.* David says *why don't you have a cup of tea and see how you get on?* David was up early to go for a walk in the hills. Olde dad had handbagged him in the hall. After a cup of tea the crisis was nearly past. The doctor was forgotten but I had to go to the chemists for pills (olde dad calls it the pharmacy for extra gravitas). I said *let's push the boat out and have another cuppa.* Olde dad takes two types of pills. One called Somethingaprazzle which is for his stomach; the other is an ibuprofen type pain-killer for his shoulder which aches now and again. I tell him he's got a bad shoulder because he sits around all day and a bad tummy because he eats shit. I try and phrase it nicer than that. But he wants to be taking pills. He is astounded and dejected that he isn't more ill than he is. Everyone of his generation is now dead – wife, brother, sister, all the family of his wife, all those uncles and aunts of mine in Manchester or Australia – all dead, all gone, and he's left with the younger generation who don't understand anything. And he isn't even ill! He's actually fighting fit. It's a scandal! He's hunting round for an illness to have. There is decline, of course there is decline, but there is no big enemy. He's involved in a skirmish but he wants a battle. The other day he went to the dentist. The dentist said *what's the problem?* Olde dad said *I've got a bad shoulder.* I try imagining the look on the dentists's face. Olde dad is like Fabrice del Dongo in Stendhal's novel *La Chartreuse de Parme.* Fabrice rides all the way from Italy to a place called Waterloo to fight next to his hero Napolean but when he gets there he kind of misses the battle. Wherever he rides off to, the battle seems to have shifted on elsewhere. He sees some horses disappearing over a horizon; he hears some explosions in the distance; he spies some soldiers in fancy hats who might be generals, but he can never get himself into a centre where the key action is taking place. He is always on the margins. He's like a man who comes to the dentists with a bad shoulder.

72.

We are sitting in the living room at nine o'clock in the morning. Olde dad is having his first cup of tea. I am having my first cup of coffee. Olde dad had not yet put his teeth in. I have not yet put my eyes in.

—   You know where is bread. You know where is turkey, says olde dad.

—   Yeah. I'll just have a banana for breakfast.

—   Ah.

—   Have you got your choppers in yet?

—   What?

—   Have you got your choppers in yet?

I know olde dad's choppers don't go in till 9.30 but you've got to ask to oil the wheels of conversation.

—   You know where is bread, you know where is turkey, says olde dad again, as though it is some saying of the ancient world.

—   Ah, I say.

—   What are you having for breakfast?

—   I'll just have a banana.

—   What time is it?

—   Half-past nine.

—   Ah! What are you having for breakfast?

—   I'll just have a banana.

—   Have honeyhoops.

—   A banana's all right for me. I think I might have another cup of coffee though. Push the boat out.

David comes down from the bathroom.

—   You had breakfast? asks olde dad.

—   I had some toast.

—   You know where is bread, you know where is turkey.

David asks me: What are you having?

—   I'll just have a banana, I say.

My olde dad, when he was in his eighties, used to listen to what he called his cassette every night before going to bed. If you were staying with him sitting in the living room at 11 o'clock you had to put up with this cassette, which you may have liked on first hearing but over time you came to execrate. It was Sarah Brightman (is that her name?) singing a selection of popular numbers, arias from popular opera or so-called classic ballads. Sarah Brightman has a fragile voice that she deploys in a pure, innocent style, as if butter wouldn't melt in her mouth. Then, one Christmas, someone (one of my sisters, not sure which one) had the bright idea of buying for olde dad a DVD of Sarah Brightman live in concert. We put it on some time on Christmas afternoon. There was Sarah Brightman dressed up in thigh-length leather boots engaged in a highly choreographed kitsch rendering of those 'classics' sexed up for modern tastes. There were provocative dance moves with a troupe of semi-naked male dancers wearing leather gilets and ticket inspector caps. They were ticket inspector caps but no tickets were being inspected, as far as I could make out. It was soon clear that in the interim between the production of that cassette and DVD technology Sarah Brightman had become a gay icon. Olde dad was bemused. What had been an angelic voice from the ether had now become the whore of Babylon. *O tempus O mores.* I don't know what happened to that DVD.

74.

In our house we eat Christmas dinner about five. This is because we have eaten egg and bacon about eleven. This means that we put the turkey in the oven about one. Liz said she wanted to do the vegetables. She lives on the other side of Manchester. *So* I said, *what time's she coming round? Dinner time* was the answer. *Does she know when dinner time is?* I said. Olde dad says she's coming round at half-past. *Half-past what?* I said. Olde dad changes his tack. *Half-past eleven,* he says. It is now three fifteen. *Which eleven?* I say. *Half past eleven in the morning or half past eleven at night?* I say. *Half past eleven in the morning,* he says. *But that was five hours ago.* Olde dad says she must be late. Anyway, Liz is here now. She won't touch sprouts, though. I'm the only one who actually likes sprouts. *When do you put the veg on?* We all look at the clock. Time gets very hard at Christmas. *That depends when the bird'll be ready.* I opened the wine with the idea that the bird would be done at five. *It's Gevrey Chambertin,* I say. *It was Napolean's favourite wine.* Nobody is much impressed. *It'll be ready when it's ready,* says Helen. Olde dad nods. That's the most sensible thing anyone's said all day.

Where's my hat? says olde dad. He has taken to wearing a hat at all times. It started when the barber cut too much off but he has continued with it. It has become olde dad's fashion statement. He looks pretty good in it, I must admit. It is woollen, a kind of toque, that he pulls up high on the head to give himself a layer of warm air between the top of his head and the interior of the hat. *Do you go up to bed in it?* I ask. *I may have it in the bathroom*, he says. In his hat he looks like the Renaissance portrait of a Medici banker or the top dog of some Dominican monastery. There is a Bellini portrait of *Fra Teodoro of Urbino as St Dominic* painted in 1515, one of his last paintings, that comes to mind, with the toque and the three-quarters profile. There is a photo of olde dad with the toque on that particularly recalls the Bellini portrait. The idea behind the pursed lips of Fra Teodoro is that he is giving nothing away. It is a quality that olde dad has always had in photos. There is one from about five years ago with me and him sitting together next to the bins that I call *two old duffers near bins* where he has the same pursed lips and distrustful look towards the camera. Even the pictures of his younger self betray the same distrust. I remember for some reason I showed a picture of him to my friend Jenny-Paule in Paris many years ago and she said to me *Tu ne passeras pas* (thou shalt not pass) and I asked what she meant and she said he was giving nothing away. I hadn't really seen it before. Now it's the only thing I see.

I have laid my bed out on the living room floor ready for sleep. Olde dad is about to go up. Suddenly he notices the bedding on the floor. *Who sleeps here*, he says, *on the living room floor?* He looks across to me with urgent concern. I look back at him. *Who do you think?* I say. He looks down and reflects. Who could it be? he is thinking. After a good thirty seconds he has sorted it out. *You*, he says. *That's right*, I say. *I know my place.* He nods. He doesn't know things now. He works them out. He goes up. Two minutes later he comes down. *Forgot something?* I say. *Forgot to take this off*, he says. He pulls off his jumper. *Don't you do that upstairs with the other clothes?* I say. *Nah*, he says. *I do this downstairs. And I need a drink.* He goes into the kitchen and comes back with some colourless liquid. *Water?* I say. *Lemonade*, he says. *Ah*, I say. He puts it down on the little table next to his armchair. *Right. I'm off*, he says. He is leaving the full glass of lemonade behind. *Aren't you having your lemonade?* I say. *I leave it there for the night*, he says. He will be striding over me in the night to get to it. *Don't you want to take it up with you?* I say. *You could put it next to your bed on that little table.* Olde dad tuts. *Nah*, he says. *Night.*

77.

Living with my olde dad is like playing an extended game of noughts and crosses. The moves you have at your disposal are limited; there is no real scope for any creativity; you just try and go through the game to the eventual statement and then start again. We have created a little walk round the block (the walk to the supermarket is too long for him now). We go out onto Town Lane and turn left, we go past *Bargain Booze* and olde dad says *Ah Bargain Booze* and I say *yes it used to be Costcutters, didn't it.* Then we turn onto a path across a field and I say *look at those trees blowing* and olde dad stares straight ahead and I say *no up there* and he raises his head and says *Ah. It's blowy up there*, I say. Then we turn down around past a house where the first day there was a woman in her garden and olde dad said to her *nice day* (it was blowing a gale and raining and he wasn't joking; he was just issuing a standard remark from his stock with no adapting to reality). Then we go up a road called Melbourne street and I say *do you know what country Melbourne is in* and olde dad doesn't know so I say *it's a big city in Australia* and he goes *Ah.* And then there's another street and olde dad reads it and it's Shoecroft Street and he says *where's that?* and I say *I don't know if that's a town.* And then we get back onto Town lane and olde dad stops in front of a new-build block of flats and says it used to be a shop. I say *Ah* but I'm not sure he's right. Then he reads the name of a hairdresser next to *Bargain Booze: Inspire Hair by Emma.* Olde dad says *it's a hairdressers* and I say *just for women* and olde dad says *no, it's for men too.* I ask *do you go there?* though I know he doesn't and he says he doesn't know and then adds *yes.* The shutters are up and I say *I'm not sure if it's still open* and then I add, *maybe she's on holiday.* And then we turn back onto our street and if the sun is out we say *let's get on the sunny side.* Then we get back and olde dad opens the front door which he had not locked. We get back in and it's who gets to the toilet first.

Between waking and sleeping is an indeterminate zone where thoughts spin in uncontrollable eddies. Sometimes, you catch yourself unawares in this whirlpool. You think you are awake, but then as you emerge from the vortex, you have an instant where you recall the chaos but realise you had been in that antechamber between sleep and waking. It is like this for olde dad a lot now. What he utters are wisps of the unconscious, unspoken preoccupations, elfin things. A conversation with him is like the meeting of two species communicating across centuries.

Yesterday I was trying to talk to him about going to the barber. His hair has got long and his eyebrows are ferocious. He couldn't find the word 'eyebrow'; it kept coming out as 'strawberry tart'. He eats many strawberry tarts in a day. If there are six in the fridge he will eat all six. Strawberry tart has become the deepest, most emblematic embodiment of his heart's desire.

I asked him what year it was. He muttered for a few moments and then said it was the sixth century. I asked him what month it was. He didn't know. I said *is it summer or winter?* He said it was neither. I said *what's that over there* (pointing at the Christmas tree)? He examined it and couldn't make it out. He looked again and said it was a tree. I said *it's a Christmas tree.* I said *It was Christmas a few days ago.* He nodded a bit but I'm not sure if, at that moment anyway, he knew what I meant.

Vassia said olde dad was eating a fruit and nut chocolate bar. He ate it but took out all the raisins and the nuts so that he had a handful of nuts and raisins in his hand, holding them out to be seen like Jack with the beans that he got in exchange for the cow, the beans that would eventually become the beanstalk, beans that really were magic, tokens that really were worth their weight in gold. He looked at them and said *how do I reckon them up?* Vassia asked him what he meant and he said *how do I know if I'm winning or losing?*

And Vassia said, *it's not a game, grandad, it's a chocolate bar.*
We cut grandad's hair and he said he felt like a new man. He called for a mirror. *I feel like a new man. A new man with a gun.* He makes a rhyme for everything now. *What a mistake-a to make-a!* he says. *Ten o'clock knock knock.* He put some gloves on. They're tight, I said, as we equipped him as though for an arctic expedition (he is walking up to the bus stop and back with David). *Tight like a mite,* he says.

The body is an undiscovered country every day. A sore on the back that had mysteriously emerged some time ago has now disappeared. Hair on the legs gone; now they are smooth. The elastic on the sock has left a deep channel above the ankle. The nails are like trees from some magic forest in Lord of the Rings. One eye has gone small. And yet within it all, all this ageing, I catch a side view of an expanse of cheek, its sheen young and fresh.

Today we see he has two pairs of trousers on. Where have his new pyjamas gone? They are nowhere to be seen. Not under the bed which is where stuff sometimes lodges. Or in his cupboard. A few weeks ago Helen had put her underwear out on the landing. It disappeared. It transpired olde dad was wearing her knickers. Today he has two pairs of trousers on, one on top of the other. I don't know how he even managed to pull the outer pair up over the inner pair. To do that would be like one of the Labours of Hercules.

Olde dad comes back from walking with David to the bus stop. David has gone back now. He's back at work tomorrow so he has to go back on the Sunday even before the festive engineering works have stopped on the railway line, which means he's taking the coach. Good luck! When olde dad got back he suddenly had a thing about shoes. *Where are all my shoes?* he said. *You've only got one pair of shoes, dad,* Helen said. I think that's true. I wouldn't see why he'd have more than one pair of shoes. Olde dad is having none of that. He goes hunting round the living room looking at shoes. *They're mine, dad,* I say as he hunches over one pair. *Pull the settee out,* he says. He wants to get at the cupboard under the stairs. *We're not pulling that settee out,* says Helen. *I looked in the cupboard before Christmas. There are no shoes in there.* Olde dad is unhappy for five minutes. He wants the settee pulled out. Then he's forgotten about the shoe trove under the stairs. *Has David been talking about shoes?* we ask, furious, as though this was the last thing for anyone to bring up to the surface. A few minutes later olde dad is trying on Vassia's doc martins. Vassia is fourteen. *Those are Vassia's,* I say. *They're not yours dad. You've never had a pair of doc martins. You've only got one pair of shoes.* Olde dad looks at me, as if realising that this must be true and that he must be and must always have been that kind of person, the kind of person that would only have one pair of shoes. I am suddenly but only for a moment ashamed of the boxes and boxes of shoes that I have in my spare room at home.

When I was a thirteen years old I was still wetting my bed at night. Not every night but quite often. My mum and dad didn't mention it much so as not to stress me out. Once my brother taunted me with it and threatened to tell my friends at school, but mostly he was pretty good about it too. After a bit the bed-wetting just stopped. I can't think what it was all about. I wasn't highly stressed as a child, I was confident, outgoing, extrovert, popular. I don't know what I had to be troubled about. Maybe it was just a weak bladder.

Now the shoe is on the other foot. Olde dad is doing the wet in the bed and we are thinking how to deal with it. First, he has to accept it. He keeps denying, saying no. The other day he went into Vassia and Natasha's room early in the morning and said, *It's terrible out, I'm wet through*. He had wet himself, but fifteen minutes later was in denial. Tonight we are trying to get him to wear a waterproof couche under his pyjamas. I'm telling him it's his special Christmas underpants. I know he won't buy this but we'll give it a go. The wheel has come full circle. I am not there to help with this. I live 200 miles away. My poor sister has to change the sheets every morning until he accepts to wear the bedpants. This morning she sent me a text. *Just got up. Dad been up all night. Eaten four strawberry tarts and virtually a whole loaf cake in the night. He's sitting in his chair with his coat and shoes on. At least the bed isn't wet this morning.* He's got shoes; he's got a coat; but he doesn't go out anymore. Out is finished. Now there's just in.

When I spoke to my sister Liz on the phone today and asked my usual question *How's the old man going?* she said *he's getting worse.* She came back from holiday and went over to see him. Liz lives on the other side of Manchester. He took her up to the end of the house and showed her the view down through to the extension at the back and the French windows that look out onto the small back garden. This was what he had done for me last time and asked me to admire it. *Yes, I know,* I said to Liz, *and then he says it's the best house in Denton.* But Liz said *no, this time he said 'I did that'.* And Liz said *what do you mean, you did that?* And olde dad said *I did it. I built that extension.* And Liz said *no you didn't, dad. It was that man Nigel, Dimitris' friend. It was Nigel who came and built the new kitchen and the new extension.* And olde dad shook his head and said *oh no, I made it. I did it.*

In a museum devoted to prehistoric life in Canada one exhibit is a slab of purple-black rock with a slender orange line that runs through it. The orange line is a geological marker for the huge asteroid that smashed into the earth at the time of the dinosaurs, obliterated them and practically everything that was and changed everything forever. The force of the asteroid was a billion times greater than the atom bomb that hit Hiroshima. Scientists say that that orange line separates the Mesozoic age from the Cenozoic age.

The idea that olde dad believes that he built the new kitchen and the extension is like crossing that orange line. It is a step change in his behaviour. He has crossed the orange line from Mesozoic to Cenozoic. He is stepping onto new territory now.

FOUR

171 Movies on Sky

When over months and years the process of diminishment has gone on, what remains is only a fragment of what once was and so it is easier to let go of.

Dimitris told me that once or twice in the night when he came down he had found him on the floor. By this time dad was up practically all night. He had stopped wearing his hat, forgotten about it. And then one day when he was trying to sit down in his armchair he sat on the arm and fell onto the wooden floor where he hit his head. It knocked him out and when Helen saw it she ran over. He was suddenly, immediately, snoring. After a few moments he came to and seemed all right, but after a few minutes it was clear he wasn't. She phoned for the ambulance and he was taken to Stepping Hill hospital. The ambulance workers wanted to take him to Tameside hospital but Helen managed to convince them to go to Stepping Hill instead as it was there Liz worked as a nurse. This was Saturday. Helen phoned me on Sunday and we said we'd play it by ear for me coming back. He seemed all right. When the nurse asked him his name he'd said 'Georgie Porgie'. Another rhyme to go with the rest. Little charms. The wisdom of a lifetime.

On Monday night nobody called me, so I assumed it was all right. On Tuesday morning about eight I phoned and Helen said it wasn't looking good. The doctors had said he had had a massive heart attack and had pneumonia. I went to Euston and got the next train up to Manchester. Dimitris met me at Stockport station. We waited for David to arrive a few minutes later and then we went to Stepping Hill. Dad was in a bed in a ward of older men. The curtains were all drawn around his bed. Helen and Liz and Vassia were sitting around the bed. There was an oxygen mask on his mouth and nose. He was breathing heavily with great difficulty. David went round one side and held his right hand and I held the left hand. Dad's eyes were open wide. In fact, they never blinked over the next few hours. His mouth was open. From time to time we applied a tiny sponge soaked with water and stuck on the end of a little stick to his lips. We pushed it gently into his mouth and he brought his lips down over it to extract some water. He had hardly eaten since coming into the hospital on Saturday. Sometimes we addressed him directly to try and elicit a response but there was little reaction. From time to time he kicked the sheet off to expose his legs and kick with them, lifting them up and into the air. We said *he's doing his exercises.* We said *look at those legs. Look how smooth the skin is and how slender they are.* I said to Liz: *I bet you wish you had legs like that.* It was a graceful movement, like a dragonfly or daddy-longlegs delightfully kicking its legs into the air. Sometimes we chatted amongst ourselves. After lunchtime Olivia, Liz's daughter, arrived from school. Now we were seven around the bed. I went down to the café with Vassia and Olivia and we had a drink and I had a sandwich. I went to the toilets which were in the Bobby Moore Unit. I don't know why it was called the Bobby Moore unit. He'd been a cockney and all his teams had been down south. Maybe it was a different Bobby Moore. When we got back up to the ward the fight for breath was getting harder.

At one stage I saw how, when stretching his legs out, dad placed one ankle delicately over the other, as though a minor adjustment for optimal comfort. It is what I do in bed. How do you explain that? Can such a tiny gesture be genetic? When I automatically make that minuscule adjustment now I think of dad in his last bed.

Sometimes when we weren't trying to elicit a response from dad and when the conversation between us had fallen silent, my eyes inevitably would alight on the TV screen behind and above the bed. It was silent but it was flashing up images about how much internet browsing you could do, how you could watch Premiership football and how many films you would have access to with a simple swipe of your credit card. There were, I recall, 171 films available that Tuesday afternoon.

At about 5 o'clock we settled on a plan. Dimitris and I would stay by the bed for a few hours and Helen and David would go home for some rest. They would come back again about nine and spend the night with dad in the hospital. Everybody left. Dimitris and I watched for a time. Dad's breathing was getting heavier. Sometimes he pulled the oxygen mask away from his face as if trying to break free. After a minute or two I put it back on and he accepted it. I had noticed that at intervals the breathing was stopping and his diaphragm was still. This lasted for just a few seconds before the heavy breathing picked up again. Dimitris said he was going down to buy some drinks. I said fine. I waited next to the bed with my hand in my dad's. His grip was feeble. After a few minutes there was sudden panic. Dad was fighting. He made some sounds but he did not have the strength to be loud. I held his hand firmer. He emitted some more strangled cries. Then he clenched his teeth together and his face turned red. I understood that this might be the end. I thought about getting the nurse but then I thought that if he was dying it would be better with me. He struggled some more, making ineffectual movements with his hands. He had pulled his hand away from me. It was his own struggle now. I felt there was ruination happening inside. Then, with as much shifting as his strengthless body would allow, he wriggled restlessly in the bed and gave out what seemed to be a final suffocated sound and lay still. The heavy breathing of his diaphragm had stilled. It was still. I waited for a few seconds. Then I approached my hand and placed my palm on his stomach. When I did so he started again; the same final suffocated cry and stirring. For a few seconds. Then he was still again. I waited. I placed my palm on his belly again. This time nothing. He was dead. I waited for a minute. I raised my head from the body. There behind the bed was the television screen showing on an endless silent reel Sergio Aguero putting the ball in the back of the net for Man City, the net rippling and the seething mass of the crowd in ecstasy behind the goal. I got up and emerged from the curtains. The life of the ward was going on. I called the nurse. I said I think it's finished. She came into the area with me and said yes. *Poor thing*, she said. She tried to close his eyes and pulled the sheets up neatly over the body. I came out of the curtained area again and phoned Helen. *Yes?* she said. *It's happened*, I said.

83.

Jacqueline's Broken Glasses

In the house now olde dad's hat is in the bathroom lying on a surface. The armchair he sat on downstairs has been pushed against the wall and rotated slightly so that now it looks out obliquely at the events of the living room. David now sits where olde dad used to sit at the dinner table. Small items still lie on tables or chests-of-drawers around the house but there isn't much. Natasha's boyfriend Den, who could not make the funeral, has requested an item. We don't know what to give him. Helen thinks we could give him a pair of olde dad's glasses which are now just staring out into nowhere from olde dad's coffee table, the space where he put his satellite objects: cups, plates, glasses, squares of chocolate. At the hospital I gathered up the personal effects and put them in a plastic bag to take home. Teeth; half a block of Galaxy; a comb; a cardigan. Back at the house Helen has stripped olde dad's bed. The mattress will be thrown away. I tell Dimitris the council might take it, along with the old armchair, for a small fee. That's how it is in Lambeth anyway. In the last few days at home dad was not even eating strawberry tarts anymore.

We phoned everyone. The Serbian and Bosnian connection were unable to come to the funeral at such short notice because of visas. Young Joe, uncle Joe's son, couldn't come because he is unwell. Cousin Chris was going to come on his motorbike from Northampton but he left a message saying he'd been up till 4.30 in the morning sick, so he didn't come. We phoned Jacqueline in Australia. She was our cousin and when we were little she lived with us. I remember throwing her glasses across the bedroom the day before she started secondary school and them breaking. Jacqueline was especially concerned about what the Headmaster of her new school, Mr Mullan, would think of her turning up at St Michael's on the first day with a pair of broken spectacles. *Mr Mullan'll murder me*, she said. I was five. I was laughing. She would have gone in to that first day at big school with some sellotape around the frame. This was a common look at the time. Jacqueline is now a social worker in Perth working with the courts. I hadn't spoken to her for decades.

The grave was deeper than I had remembered. It was mum's grave and we lowered olde dad's coffin down by the straps on top of it. A photo of dad as a handsome young man had been transported from the house to the church where it was placed on the coffin, then ferried to the cemetery in the hearse. Now it was shipped back home and put back on the chest of drawers with the cards and flowers.

Helen had ordered sandwiches and pies and cakes and some fruit from Martins, the new bread and confectioner's shop that had recently set up in the old market square. The pork pies were especially good. There were a couple of bottles of wine available and some beer but it was mostly cups of tea. I had a small glass of sherry and some people had a spot of brandy with coke.

Natasha, who had sung an Andrea Boccelli song in the church, went back to Newcastle where she is a student at six o'clock. Vassia and Olivia read out prayers. I went back to London on the 7.55 train with David and my friend Christina who had known olde dad a few years earlier. The journey was delayed near Stoke due to a broken-down train. The ticket inspector said we could get money back because it was over 30 minutes delay but there's still no sign of any money coming back into my account.

84.

In the Bed

I slept in my dad's bed for the first time last night. Helen
had cleaned the mattress, treated it. I put my nose up
close to it. It didn't smell of urine There wasn't much in
my dad's room. It was what we used to call the box room.
There was the single bed, a thin cupboard and another
cupboard blocked into the wall. In the thin free-standing
cupboard there were dad's clothes. Most of them he never
wore. Some of the pullovers and tops, Christmas presents,
had never been unpacked from cellophane, their card
inserts still doing their job up the back of the tops. In
the cupboard that was blocked into the wall some jackets
were jammed. On the windowsill there was an old crucifix
ornament, a small photo of my mum with my granny from
the 1970s and a keyring-size photo of Olivia, my niece, as a
toddler. There are no other personal effects. My dad had no
possessions. The tattered dictionary he had once owned,
the sole remnant of his earlier life, had long since been
thrown out.

85.

Translated

Some people hoard within what you might call an identifying story about themselves. It is the story they bring out when they meet people and want to set up some kind of intimacy, the story they believe reveals the most about themselves. This is mostly a melancholy procedure. You may have already heard their identifying story and you pass by them at a party or in a gathering and you hear shards of it drifting out from a conversation they are involved in. He's telling his identifying story again. This is a dead story. It has solidified and is so often nothing more than a sentimental version of the self, stored up inside to deceive the self and others.

In 'Citizen Kane' the journalist believes he can pluck the heart out of James Foster Kane by unravelling the mystery of his last spoken word, the word 'Rosebud'. He fails, though we the audience see that 'Rosebud' was the name of the young Kane's sleigh which he had left behind as a child on the day he was taken away for his destiny of wealth and power.

As we grow older childhood becomes a distant land where a stranger lived, a stranger that was you. They tell you it was you. It must be you. But can you really accept what they say? Olde dad looked back to a land of mist and fable, an old fairy tale he once half-read. There are the outlines of a landscape; the shapes of a village as seen through squinting eyes in blinding light; the silhouette of a woman who may have been his mother. All so remote now. They have spiralled away, light years away.

And what was the Rosebud moment? The pinprick of sharp light that might yield a spark that might yield a metaphor that might yield a meaning, though never a true meaning like Rosebud. Rosebud wasn't the life. The life was the accumulation of all the stuff, the grand aggregate. So many things that there can be no simple yield. It is this pile, the life. Its meanings rifle out in all directions, bewildering. You cannot control them.

I am imagining my dad as a very young man. The moment he steps across the frontier, the moment he escapes from his native land, his first land. It is night. There is a moon in the sky. There are stars in the heavens. It is so late it is early. There is dew on the grass. He steps across the dew. There is a new world waiting for him out there. The war is coming to an end but things have changed. There has been a tilt in the landscape and everything has been re-jigged. Beyond the spur in the hills, over the pass, is a new life. He steps forward. Each step brings him closer to safety. The stars are dissolving into the morning sky. Constellations shine in his young man's eyes. There are other figures beside him. Other men who will never go back. The dust is on his heavy boots. The dew will wash them clean. He steps from one world into another.

Then, suddenly, from one moment to the next, it is as if there is a sudden break-down in the current, one of those moments where the electricity snaps off for just a moment and you all look round at each other and say *what just happened?* And you realise there has been a tiny power cut for whatever technical reason that you will never know about. So that nothing has changed and you get on with your life. Except that when you look at some things, some settings, some ways that things had always worked up till then, some stuff to do with your computer maybe, everything has been wiggled around, readjusted somehow. And when the young man re-assumes shape an infinitesimal instant later, he too is translated, his world is different. He is leaving the old life behind and emerging into a new one. What happened in that moment, that space, we do not know, we cannot guess.